1179

Puffin Books
*Editor: Kaye Webb*

GW00864820

# Great Escapes
A Collection of Escape Stories

# Great Escapes

## A COLLECTION OF ESCAPE STORIES

EDITED BY DAVID HOWARTH

PUFFIN BOOKS
in association with Hamish Hamilton

Puffin Books, Penguin Ltd,
Harmondsworth, Middlesex, England
Penguin Books, 625 Madison Avenue,
New York, New York 10022, U.S.A.
Penguin Books Australia Ltd, Ringwood,
Victoria, Australia
Penguin Books Canada Ltd, 2801 John Street,
Markham, Ontario, Canada L3R 1B4
Penguin Books (N.Z.) Ltd, 182–190 Wairau Road,
Auckland 10, New Zealand

First published by Hamish Hamilton 1969
Published in Puffin Books 1979

Copyright © Hamish Hamilton, 1969
All rights reserved

*The Acknowledgements on page 208
constitute an extension of this copyright page*

Made and printed in Great Britain by
C. Nicholls & Company Ltd
Set in Linotype Pilgrim

Except in the United States of America, this book is
sold subject to the condition that it shall not, by
way of trade or otherwise, be lent, re-sold, hired
out, or otherwise circulated without the publisher's
prior consent in any form of binding or cover other
than that in which it is published and without
a similar condition including this condition
being imposed on the subsequent purchaser

# CONTENTS

# EDITOR'S FOREWORD

*Escape!* It is a word that first makes you think of breaking out of fortresses or prisons, and running away from people who are hunting you. Perhaps it especially makes you think of prisoners of war, tunnelling under barbed-wire fences or inventing cunning ways to deceive their guards, and travelling in disguise through enemy countries.

But there are other kinds of escape too. You may have to escape from circumstances, not from human enemies: from the sea, for example, or from mountains, or from the Arctic ice – from any situation where you cannot continue to live. And to make your escape, you do not always have to run away, or even to move at all: you may have to do it just by staying where you are, and holding on, and keeping yourself alive until the circumstances change. Sometimes, that is the hardest escape of all.

There are all kinds of escapes in this collection. The classic example of the prisoner-of-war story is Winston Churchill's escape from the Boers. There are also three stories of escapes in World War II, which I have included because they are unusual. Gladys Aylward's trek across China with a hundred children shows that you do not have to be a he-man to achieve a great escape: you may be impelled to it by compassion, and carry it through by nothing but stubborn determination. Captain Jennings's story began as an escape from the Japanese, but turned into an escape from a deadlier enemy, and led to what I believe is the longest journey ever made in an open boat. And Odd Starheim's story is certainly unusual too. I am glad to say I knew Odd Starheim, and I do not know anyone else who would have thought, when he had to escape, of stealing a large passenger ship to do it in.

When does an escape become a rescue? You might say that Admiral Byrd was rescued from his hut in the Antarctic, and so he was in the sense that his colleagues went to fetch him. But his was a supreme example of escaping by doing nothing – merely by deciding not to die, and keeping alive for week after week, in the face of disaster and disappointment, and in the depth of mental and physical distress.

I know many men who have had to escape, from circumstances or from human enemies, or from both at once. And I have known many who were unlucky, and failed to escape, and died, as Starheim did in the end. If I ask the survivors what it was that kept them going, they always find it difficult to answer. Other people can call it courage. But those who have been through it do not use that kind of word: they were lucky, they say, and – well – they just didn't think the time had come to die.

David Howarth

# E. O. HAUGE

# The Man who Stole a Ship

Odd Starheim was a Norwegian who was twenty-four when
the Germans invaded and occupied his country in 1940. He
escaped to England for training, and then went back to the
south of Norway and set up a large and successful spy
organization against the occupying forces. For a long time,
he sent information to England by a radio transmitter
hidden in the attic of a farm. He sent the news that the
German battleship *Bismarck* was sailing towards the Atlantic
– and the Royal Navy intercepted and sank her. He warned
Britain that the Germans were manufacturing heavy water
in Norway, a component of atomic bombs – and a commando
party raided the heavy-water plant.

It was a life of hairbreadth escapes, and one of them
came when he was staying in Oslo with a member of his
organization called Korsvig Rasmussen.

Early next morning, he was shaken awake by Mrs Rasmussen
in a state of terror; the police had arrived to arrest her husband.
They were searching the flat; 'Ola Svendsen' must escape – if
there was still time.

Starheim leapt out of bed, seized a dressing-gown and made
for the bathroom. Before he could reach it a policeman appeared at the door and stopped him. Next instant two Germans
entered his room, obviously delighted by this additional catch.
In the circumstances they rightly guessed that Korsvig Rasmussen's guest might very probably be someone of importance.
Starheim made every effort to collect his thoughts and think
quickly; he had determined long ago not to live if the Germans
were to catch him; he therefore proposed trying every possible
means of escape before coming to the final conclusion. It was
most unfortunate that they should have surprised him in bed:
in all other circumstances he had his revolver and 'L' tablets on
him; in his pyjamas he had neither.

A German officer asked him for his identity card. Starheim walked to the chair where his coat was hanging and took the papers he had acquired in Flekkefjord from the pocket. The German examined them and concluded that the papers of Ola Svendsen, sailor, were genuine enough; then asked what Herr Svendsen was doing in Oslo. Starheim had his cover story and proceeded to explain. As though overcome with nerves, he began raising his voice; he had arrived the previous evening from Flekkefjord, where he had signed off a German vessel; he was visiting Oslo to see a specialist about his stomach complaint – the doctor's certificate was produced – he had found on reaching Oslo that all the hotels were filled with delegates from all over the country arriving for the National Front Congress which Quisling was holding in the Capital. He had wandered all over the city and was disconsolately making up his mind to spend the night out in the public gardens, when whom should he meet, walking down the Karl Johan Avenue, but Herr Rasmussen, whom he had known slightly before the war in Flekkefjord; he had explained his position and Herr Rasmussen had kindly offered him a bed.

All the while Starheim had been talking the door into the drawing-room stood ajar, and he hoped that Korsvig, who was sitting there being interrogated by another German officer, would be able to hear all he had said and make his answers accordingly.

There were in all five members of the police in the flat – two Norwegians and three German Gestapo officials. They refused, rather naturally, to accept Starheim's story at its face value, and ordered him to get ready to accompany them to Gestapo headquarters at 19 Mollergata for further interrogation.

A policeman took up his stand in the open doorway and Starheim began to dress. The other police officials started searching the flat. The only objects which they seemed to find compromising were a portrait of the royal family and a book which had been banned in Norway since the occupation.

Starheim was taking as long as possible to dress, his mind running over the alternatives that remained to him. He felt

sure his best chance of escape would be during the moments
that remained before the whole party left the flat; once on
their way to the Gestapo headquarters with five armed men
watching him, a getaway would be next to impossible.

The door of his room guarded by the policeman was still
open. Mrs Rasmussen came in as though to ask if she could
help; on the belief that the policeman at that moment was not
observing him, Starheim nodded in the direction of the window.
Mrs Rasmussen was completely collected, understood him instantly and, seeing that her guest was dressed and ready to go
out, made as though to open the window to air the room. However this housewifely little move – it was still nearly pitch dark
outside and bitter cold – was spotted at once by the policeman
and intercepted. He left his post at the door, pushed Mrs Rasmussen aside and planted himself in front of the window,
machine-gun at the alert. Mrs Rasmussen registered injured in-
nocence and hovered around the next room while Starheim
went on collecting the last oddments of his clothing. His original
idea, the bathroom, was now his only hope; he had after all,
intimated that he suffered from a stomach complaint; he pol-
itely asked the policeman if he might go to the w.c. Even without a stomach complaint, at that hour of the morning, it was a
natural request. Starheim eyed the man, wondering if he would
swallow the bait. The policeman adopted an impatient frown
and nodded. As Starheim left the room and made for the w.c. he
noticed that the machine-gun and its bearer were following him.
He entered rapidly, locked the door and waited; there was nothing whatever the matter with his tummy and he had much more
urgent needs to attend to. There was a second door to the w.c.
which opened straight into the bedroom used by Mrs Rasmussen's mother. Starheim hoped and prayed it might not be locked
on the other side. He changed the position of his revolver from
the pocket under his armpit to his right-hand hip pocket. When
he judged he had waited long enough he pulled the plug de-
cisively, and put his hand softly on the latch of the second door.
The water was making a goodly noise; the latch yielded, the door
opened; Starheim ran through the old lady's room. She was
trembling in bed in silent terror. He had no time to speak; flung

open the window, took no first look but climbed straight on to the sill and leapt out into the darkness.

He fell fourteen feet and landed on a smooth, ice-covered boulder on his right heel, spraining it severely. As his eyes got accustomed to the darkness he was able to make out two police cars at the front entrance of the house. He picked himself up, ran across the garden, jumped over the fence and tore down the high road towards the centre of the city as fast as he had ever run in his life. He could see a car coming towards him; as it drew nearer it turned out to be a lorry. Starheim stopped; braced himself, sprang on to the running-board, and shouted to the driver, 'Are you a good Norwegian?'

'Yes,' replied the driver without turning his head. 'Who is chasing you – Germans?' he added, presumably hoping he was not abetting a common thief.

'The Gestapo!' said Starheim. The driver looked him in the eye for an instant and shouted, 'Jump in!' – in his best English, the more to honour the occasion. Though wartime petrol restrictions demanded that this vehicle should be run on charcoal gas, Starheim quickly understood that the wild rate at which the engine accelerated could only have been managed with real petrol in the tank. They rattled down side roads, ascertained they were not followed and ended up in the home of the excellent driver. Starheim was given every assistance and no questions were asked. Neither man introduced himself to the other, though they lived together for two days, at the end of which time Starheim had acquired a new false passport under the name of Ola Steenvold, had warned his friends, cancelled further meetings and arranged to make the attempt to get out of Oslo in the most brazen way he could devise – by train to Kristiansand.

So far so good. But Rasmussen was held by the Gestapo. There was a risk he might be forced to talk, and Starheim and his organization might be discovered. Starheim had to get out of the country, and he thought of an original plan to do so; to steal one of the passenger ships which run up and down the Norwegian coast. Two men of his organization, named Fasting and Skinnarland, joined him in the plot, and a ship's engineer and two stokers offered to help.

S.S. *Galtesund*, 620 tons, belonged to the Arendal Steamship Company. She carried a complement of seventeen men, two stewardesses and two permanent pilots. The question of anti-aircraft guns had been mooted many months earlier, but no one was particularly anxious to have the German gun crew on board, so the matter had now been expedited by the captain, who had announced without enthusiasm that the guns would be ready waiting to be mounted when they reached Stavanger next day. Starheim had travelled on the *Galtesund* before the war, but he had not then felt the need to make her his special study; he had an hour before him now in which to do so.

As *Galtesund* emerged from the lee of the sheltering mountains, Starheim noticed that a stiff breeze was blowing from the north-east; more snow would be on the way; all to the good. *Galtesund* passed below Hidra Foreland under the nose of bristling German defences; it was 5.45 p.m.

Starheim hurried to the poop, where the two reliable stokers were waiting under the watchful eye of their ex-chief engineer friend.

'Well, fellows,' Starheim began in what he rightly conceived to be a voice of authority, 'In exactly twenty minutes we intend to capture the *Galtesund*. We know there is enough coal on board. I am taking over command and steering for Aberdeen. I have got two determined friends in charge for'ard, and I'd like to entrust the engine-room to you.' The dumbfounded stokers only stared; Starheim went on: 'As you obviously understand, we shall be taking a risk, but I am sure all will go well. My name is Ola Steenvold, and I am a lieutenant of the Royal Norwegian Navy; are you with us?'

The two reliable stokers shuffled their feet and swallowed their silence; they would do all they could to help. Suddenly a grin spread over their faces – this was war! 'And war is no joke,' warned Starheim; 'we are risking our lives, and if the Germans catch us there can be no hope of pardon.'

The plan of action was explained in detail; the two beginners were each given a loaded pistol, which they handled with great respect; they had never touched a live firearm before. Starheim showed them the movements of the safety-catch;

there was no time for more. He counted on them carrying out their part of the action by bluff, as far as possible. If any real shooting was to be done, he would do it himself. Each man was handed a watch, which had already been synchronized. The senior of the two stokers was ordered to take charge of the off-duty crew in their bunks; he moved away to take up his station. Starheim glanced at his watch – it was 6.18 p.m.

Fasting and the engineer went slowly slouching down the deck, hands in bulging pockets, towards the door of the engine-room. Starheim put his hands into his pockets and moved slowly towards the door of the saloon, while from the other side, limping in step with his leader, Skinnarland approached the same door, his hands, too, in his pockets. On the other side of the door sat the captain and a passenger, chatting. Starheim braced his elbows, about to draw up his hands; Skinnarland placed his fingers on the handle of the door . . . from behind him came the sound of footsteps. It was the second mate abruptly asking Starheim if he had bought his ticket.

'No, I'm afraid I arrived too late – so I thought I would pay for it on board,' said Starheim.

The second mate suggested he had better come along with him at once, as he was closing down the office and wanted to get his accounts settled up. He added, 'By the way, aren't there two of you?'

Starheim's mind raced over the possibility of finishing off the second mate on the spot, but decided that the couple in the saloon would probably hear the scuffle and raise the alarm; his whole plan must hinge on securing the captain first; he therefore winked at Skinnarland and said to the second mate, 'I'll pay for both of us.' Starheim followed the man to the ship's office. A few minutes' delay might do no harm – but the other members of his party would already be in action. He produced the money for the fares and handed it over while the two tickets were briskly detached from the packet and put into his hand. He retraced his steps towards the saloon door; he was three minutes late. Skinnarland looked at his watch, said not a word, calmly opened the door, limped in past the captain and the passenger, towards a door at the opposite end of the room which gave into the skipper's cabin. There, he turned on his heel and raised his pistols. Simultaneously, Starheim stepped into the saloon, his two pistols at the ready. 'Hands up!' he ordered.

The captain and the passenger stopped chatting; they remained seated in amazement. They knew that war had its terrors, but nothing quite so sudden had happened to them before: two young men aiming at them with four pistols which quite clearly meant business.

'We are officers of the Norwegian Navy,' said Starheim sharply. 'We are not alone; at this instant my men are seizing control in the engine-room, on deck, on the bridge. In the name of the Royal Norwegian Navy I now assume command of this ship. Everybody is to remain calm; anyone who defies my orders or who attempts sabotage will be shot instantly. The captain will be placed under arrest in his cabin. The rest of the crew will be held in the saloon under guard till further orders.'

The passenger was the first to recover his voice. 'But I'm going to a christening in Star . . .'

'Shut up!' roared Starheim, and the passenger relapsed into silence.

'I protest!' said the captain.

'No protests here,' replied Starheim sharply. 'I am now in charge of this ship and you, Captain Knudsen, as well as everyone else on board, will be obeying my orders.'

He signalled to Skinnarland, who stuffed his pistols into his pockets, limped jauntily over to the captain, took him by the scruff of the neck and propelled him into his cabin. There Skinnarland produced rope from another pocket and bound the energetically but ineffectually protesting skipper hand and foot.

Skinnarland then returned to the saloon and took over guard from Starheim, who went out to collect the second mate, who was in the act of locking up his office. With no explanation at all the petrified man was backed into the saloon and pushed on to a chair. The agonized junior stewardess was next collected off the deck and shown silently to a seat next to him. The second reliable stoker was then called in from guarding the corridor and put in charge of the saloon with his trembling pistol pointing the right way.

Starheim and Skinnarland then made for the bridge. Starheim approached the starboard door, Skinnarland the port door. The starboard door was ajar; inside stood First Mate Taraldsen and the pilot, talking; nearby stood a sailor holding the wheel. In the half-open doorway Starheim suddenly appeared with his pistols, shouting 'Hands up!'

The three men were scared stiff. The sailor dropped the helm; the first mate panicked and ran to the port door, where he met Skinnarland's pistols and changed his mind. He was ordered to turn round, and, while Starheim covered the three men with pistols, Skinnarland produced another piece of rope and neatly demonstrated again his new-won skill on the terrified Taraldsen's hands and elbows. Starheim repeated the speech he had made in the saloon and added: 'You, pilot, are now responsible, on pain of instant death, for steering a course according to my orders. The man at the wheelhouse will remain on duty until he is relieved; I am now in charge of Galtesund and shall remain on the bridge.'

The three men were still white from the shock and not one of them uttered a syllable; then Taraldsen was hurried down to the saloon at the point of Skinnarland's pistol, and Starheim, for the first time in his life, found himself in command on the bridge – master of his little world – alone.

The gradually-quickening eyes of the pilot and the sailor were upon him, but made him none the less alone. He took some strides across his bridge and tried to remember how his former captains had looked when they paced the quarterdeck, their all-powerful backs towards him, the simple sailor. His promotion had been a little rapid, perhaps; he turned, paced the whole length once again, and felt better.

'We shall now alter our course, pilot,' Starheim declared in his most impressive voice. 'West to Aberdeen. I shall myself trace the route on the chart; will you come with me into the chart-room?'

Starheim soon found that the pilot was a sensible man on whom he might rely; but even so he decided to discourage any inclination to chattiness. He understood that if a youth of his age was to control older men of longer experience, he would have to assume great determination and still greater reserve. He announced that he was expecting an escort from the R.A.F. and the Royal Navy the following morning, Sunday; he leant over the charts with an intent look on his face. 'We are now here,' said the pilot, and made a cross with his pencil.

'Right!' Starheim snapped. 'We'll now follow a line due west.' He picked up a ruler and began to trace the new course.

The pilot cleared his throat and, after murmuring that he had no intention of sabotaging or anything of that kind, said he wished to register his disagreement; it was silly to strike away from the coast at this point. 'I take it we are not supposed to be discovered by the Germans?' he asked.

'Obviously not,' answered Starheim. 'What have you in mind?'

The pilot explained that there was still enough daylight for the enemy to observe if they suddenly were to alter course; whereas if they were to continue on their normal course, they could even by-pass Rekefjord, the next scheduled port of call, without causing surprise or alarm, as the state of the ice in the fjord-mouth was known to be dangerous. If, on the other hand, the coastguards at Rekefjord should see no trace of the *Galtesund* passing by, they would be sure to report her absence. In a little over half an hour it would be too dark to see anything; the *Galtesund* could then strike away from the coast with no danger of being reported missing until the following morning.

Starheim weighed up the loss of time — a little over half an hour — the shortage of coal and the expected gain in safety by clinging to the coast yet a little longer till the night should cover their escape. He decided he would trust to the honest intentions of the pilot, and agreed as abruptly as he could; they would adhere to their present course for a further half-hour.

Starheim returned to the bridge and walked to and fro without any further talk. From time to time he took up the telescope and examined the coast, studded with enemy watchposts, all of which could see the *Galtesund* without being able to suspect that they had already lost her to England. Not another ship in sight – all quiet on the horizon. Beneath his feet he felt the familiar throbbing which is the heart-beat of all ships, and in his ears the homely purring of the engines. No shouts, no shots, no clanking to a halt; all quiet aboard.

The first act of the drama seemed to be at an end; Starheim on his bridge awaited reports.

Ship's cook Gustav Angell Sorensen was contemplating pensively the size of a sausage over which he dangled, like Damocles' sword, his carving-knife. Damocles must first calculate how many people would be wanting dinner, so he popped out into the corridor, sword in hand, to ask ... and what should he see but that odious little National Front moustache-holder darting down into the cabin of the sick ship's engineer. 'That's odd,' thought Angell Sorensen, unconsciously squaring his massive shoulders and rolling up his shirtsleeves, which disclosed already quite enough fat and muscle for any cook's arm. He was still wiping his sword across his capacious apron when Fasting darted up again, seized a jug of drinking-water from its shelf on the wall and disappeared once more into the sick man's cabin. That was odder still, thought the cook – so odd that he repaired to the deck to fetch a breath of air. The very next instant Andreas Fasting was standing beside him, poking a pistol into his beefy ribs and shouting, 'Up with the paws!' The cook formed the opinion that the little moustache-holder was rather nervous and for two pins he would have stuck that carving-knife into his throat, but it was the pistol that made him think again. Fasting grabbed at the knife and hurled it down the hatchway; he did not like the look of that cook, and it never occurred to him that his National Front button might be the cause of his unpopularity with Angell Sorensen. The cook, disarmed and deflated, was locked into his cabin.

In the engine-room the second engineer was in charge, as his chief lay ill in bed. He was rather glad than otherwise, therefore, when he heard steps on the ladder and recognized the visiting engineer toddling down. So utterly unwarlike did the visitor appear that even the pistol he cuddled gingerly took on the aspect of a toy for his little boy. The second engineer looked at it with an interested smile, and only when he realized his visitor was covered by another figure – the agile Fasting, armed to the teeth – did his smile slowly fade. But his feelings were more hurt than surprised; he had nothing at all against going to England and, of course, if he said he would keep the fires burning, he would keep them burning! He shared all the views of the ex-engineer on politics; they had had a long talk that very morning and he was in entire agreement with this latest, somewhat unexpected, development.

Leaving the two engineer colleagues together, Fasting leapt up the ladder, filled his lungs with sea-air and dashed towards the bridge to tell Starheim that everything was under control. On the way he noticed the securely-corseted little figure of the senior stewardess, tiptoeing stealthily down a passageway; Miss Johansen was tiptoeing to the horrible conclusion that something mysterious was happening on board. She realized, as any woman of her experience would have realized, that there were pirates on board the *Galtesund*. Miss Johansen was a lady of a certain age; for years the whole of the shipping company's electro-plated dining-room service on the *Galtesund* had been implicitly entrusted to her care; and she turned on the pirate and told him so in a tornado of such colourful language that Fasting, for an instant, was taken aback. The lady made good use of this momentary advantage and hurled at him a volley of naval language such as he, a mere Boy Scout and simple sailor, had never heard before. When he regained the initiative he had a most difficult and unenviable task pacifying the lady, who still insisted on guarding the company's plate with her life – her life! She shrieked again, so loudly that Fasting had not a hope of making himself heard. In time, however, she concluded that what interests she and the steamship company retained were equally well served by following this pirate to the saloon, near which the silver was in fact kept. By then the rest of the ship's company were assembled there. Much relieved, Fasting hurried on towards the bridge.

Starheim listened to his report; instructed Fasting about the latest decision in regard to the course which the pilot was to follow, and leaving his lieutenant in charge of the bridge, ran down to the saloon. To the assembled company he repeated the terse little speech he had made earlier to the captain; the *Galtesund* was now under the orders of the Royal Norwegian Navy; he, the new captain, was in touch with headquarters in London, and by the following morning an escort of aircraft and warships would be protecting them in case the Germans should discover their whereabouts. By Monday morning *Galtesund* would be safe in a British harbour; those who wished would then be free, to take an active part in the task of liberating Norway by enrolling in the Norwegian Navy or merchant fleet; those who did not wish to do so would not be impressed against their will. 'You will now have a quarter of an hour to discuss the matter among yourselves. Those of you who decide against crossing the North Sea with us will be allowed to return to Norway in a row-boat. The *Galtesund* is still near enough to the coast for that to be easily feasible.'

Starheim's absolute integrity, more than anything else, was what gave to his utterances – short and uningratiating though they were and pronounced in the strong and guttural accent of south Norway – the undeniable stamp of authority. He entered into no arguments; having nothing more to say, he turned his back on the astounded company and marched into the captain's cabin.

The elderly captain was in considerable distress. He was in no sense pro-Nazi, but was unnerved by the suddenness of events. Starheim did his best to listen patiently to him and explained, in greater detail than he had dared do in public, the action he was taking. He loosened the ropes that bound the captain and ended by stating that, in the unlikely event of the Germans overtaking them, it would be better for the captain and the whole ship's company that he should remain under arrest in his cabin; Starheim would then be solely responsible in the eyes of all concerned if things should go wrong. The captain was able to appreciate this point and agreed that he was no longer in command of his own ship. He remained, however, inconsolably pessimistic about the entire business: there would not be enough coal; they would run into minefields unless an experienced man was on the bridge; he foresaw every conceivable disaster. Finally, to comfort the poor man, Starheim agreed to keep the first mate, Taraldsen, on the bridge. Taraldsen very soon regained his good humour and did all he could to help.

A strong wind blew all through the night. Luckily the *Galtesund* was a well-built ship, but even so she rolled sufficiently for the cargo to come adrift. Starheim set all hands to stow the goods securely, then every man settled to his allotted task. On the bridge the watches took their normal turn of duty, only Starheim remained at his post throughout – he did not even feel tired. Cups of coffee and sandwiches were brought up to him, and he ate with his eyes out to sea.

As dawn broke Starheim saw that his luck had not deserted him; impenetrable clouds covered *Galtesund*. No enemy aircraft could detect her under that blanket. The hour of greatest danger was approaching: by then the ship would have been reported missing to the Germans. They would certainly order a search; aircraft would scan the normal coastal route. The question remained whether or not the enemy had heard any rumours of the capture: as soon as that idea occurred to them, their search-planes would be switched to the North Sea. A few minutes would suffice to overtake the *Galtesund*. As long as the clouds persisted the ship would be safe from the Germans. Starheim looked up to those clouds and knew they would hide him too from his R.A.F. deliverers.

With the morning came the distant sound of aircraft. Like wildfire the news spread throughout the ship; sure enough the inevitable had happened – the *Galtesund* had been discovered. Everyone came up on deck, helping one another to put on safety-jackets, while cursing in undertones Lieutenant Steenvold and his commandos. Through the covering of clouds everyone tried to tell if the sound was German or English. The 'straight' passenger recognized them as German.

On his bridge Starheim hid his mounting despair under a white, thoughtful face; he issued orders to have the boats made ready and swung clear on the davits; fresh water and ample food to be stored in each boat and everyone to take up their positions near the boat to which they had been assigned.

On his bridge, his glasses hopelessly searching the moving clouds, Starheim told himself that if German aircraft attacked the *Galtesund* there could be only the remotest chance of survival for those who took to the boats; they would row about in the middle of the North Sea, pinning their hopes on British help. How long would it take to arrive? British help must come! Had Tomstad managed to send his message? Had London received it in intelligible form? Would they act immediately? On a Saturday night – the middle of a British week-end? He would have done better to have warned them earlier about his plan ... but he had dreaded the probable objections from the Allied Commands, arguments, flat orders to desist! He had weighed it all so carefully –.but evidently in vain. He paced his bridge, kept silent and held to his resolve.

The sounds of aircraft grew fainter, returned again and then ceased. In the lull that followed Starheim ordered that part of the cargo of finest salt meat should be cut up and divided into suitable packings between the lifeboats. There was also on board the whole month's ration of tobacco for the seaports of Stavanger and Haugesund. Starheim reflected that if all went well that tobacco would soon be returning to Norway in the pockets of S.O.E. agents. The difficulty of disguising English tobacco to look and taste like the local variety had been a constant worry when preparing to dispatch men from England to the 'field'. The cargo of new furniture and mattresses, Starheim reminded himself, had been earmarked for the boiler-room – if the coal should give out.

About two o'clock in the afternoon the covering of clouds began to disperse. Shortly after, the unmistakable sounds returned Starheim heard it, the crew heard it, everyone heard it. The sounds were clearly coming up in the rear of the ship. There was nothing more to be done, save give the orders to assemble near the boats. Starheim remained on his bridge, peering into the sky in the direction of Norway.

The clouds were dispersing rapidly; the *Galtesund* would be under a clear sky in a matter of minutes – if she went on at her present rate.

It was Andreas Fasting, stationed at the poop with his glasses, who first spotted the aircraft – a long way behind the ship in the direction of Norway – a speck in the distance. Within seconds everyone knew the aircraft had been sighted. The chances were – there was no denying it – that this was a German plane. In short minutes which seemed long to them all, the aircraft would be near enough for the marks painted under the wings to be distinguishable and then, one instant more, the crash of bombs. Clinging to the railings round Fasting, they waited.

On his bridge Starheim laid aside his glasses; he would hear soon enough in any case – the black-and-silver hooked cross of the Nazis or the beloved tricolour rings of the R.A.F. He could do no more; he rested his thickly-gloved hands on the railing before him and waited – for death or life?

He saw the aircraft with his naked eye, swiftly arrive abreast the *Galtesund*, but far away to starboard; he saw it suddenly begin to swerve inwards towards the ship; like a torrent came the noise. It was a large seaplane; but both the Germans and the British used seaplanes. The roar grew louder.

Fasting, still at his post, was the first to shout, 'It's British! A Catalina!' He waved frantically with his glasses, turned, leapt down the ladder from the poop deck and scampered along the main deck, leaping over trunks and kitbags and everything that came in his way, till he reached Starheim's bridge; there he executed a wild war-dance round the telegraph apparatus.

The little knots of humanity by the boats had scattered and were wildly cheering and waving as the monstrous seaplane sailed slowly, low over the mast-tops. Jubilation reigned throughout the *Galtesund*.

On his bridge Starheim's white face showed no sign; his hands still clutched the railing. He turned his head and, in a ringing voice, gave his command: 'Break the flag aft!'

'Second mate! Prepare for signalling!'

'Inform the men below immediately!'

In the instant of silence that followed, Starheim remained motionless while the bright flag of Norway unfurled to the fresh sea wind; the greatest moment of his life was passing.

'Send the following signal' – Starheim collected himself and continued. '"*Galtesund* making for Aberdeen and want pilot."'

The seaplane was circling low over the ship; with her flash-lamp she signalled back: 'CONGRATULATIONS'. Starheim shouted aloud each blessed letter as it formed. So at last all doubt was dispelled – London, after all, had risen to the occasion. A spirit was abroad on that ship which touched every human heart present; the old captain climbed up to the bridge and joined in the glee.

In half an hour's time two fighter planes joined the seaplane and circled round the *Galtesund*, throbbing in her pride. Star-heim ordered beer to be served to the entire ship's company. The 'straight' passenger, who had missed his family reunion at Stavanger, was served with a bottle of the best wine on board.

'And who pays?' squeaked Miss Johansen.

'The Royal Norwegian Government,' replied Starheim.

One of the aircraft was making the strangest convolutions as it flew round the *Galtesund*, and, to begin with, Starheim fan-cied the airman must be playing a joke. Starheim had come to know some of the R.A.F. types during his parachute training and the long days and nights hanging around the great secret hangars before he was dispatched to Norway. He wondered what the joke could be about. Suddenly Hansen, the pilot of the *Galtesund*, declared: 'He wants us to stop.' Starheim seized the engine telegraph. How often in days gone by, when he had been serving his turn of duty in the capacity Dag Kristoffersen was serving now, he had longed to try pressing that handle; with delight he now discovered how quickly a ship reacts to that pressure. He signalled STOP. She stopped. Then once again he signalled FULL SPEED ASTERN: the *Galtesund* went back-wards. STOP! he signalled; she stopped and lay there drifting on the waves. The airman swooped down over the ship, evidently satisfied by Starheim's manoeuvres. Shortly afterwards an armed trawler appeared out of the mist, bristling with can-non and anti-aircraft guns – an escort vessel. The airman's task of bringing these two ships together had been accomplished.

The captain of the escort vessel sent a signal: once again

Starheim deciphered, létter by letter, 'CONGRATULATIONS'. Praise from the Royal Navy was praise indeed to Ola's mind. The armed trawler then led the way and *Galtesund* followed through the minefields, trusting that their destination would be Aberdeen; Starheim badly wanted it to be the same port he had come to once before.

As night fell, Starheim flung himself on the divan in the chart-room and tried to get some sleep; but sleep would not come to him. The escort ship was continually signalling alterations in the course – he must be on the bridge. By first light he heard the familiar sound of foghorns; *Galtesund* was approaching the friendly coast. He strained to see if there were some landmarks he could recognize. Two hours later, out of the mist, slowly and unmistakably, came Aberdeen lighthouse; alone, he nodded to it. Then a motor-boat came alongside; the rope ladder was let down and the harbour police came on board. Then another motor-boat with military police and the harbour pilot. Starheim walked to the starboard side, looked at his bright Norwegian flag in the crisp light of day and, for the first time since he had captured his prize, he went below to his cabin.

– from *Salt Water Thief*

# CHARLES II

# The King's Escape

One of the famous escapes of English history was made by King Charles II after his army was beaten by the army of Oliver Cromwell at Worcester in September 1661. His object was to get to France, but Cromwell had alerted the whole of England to catch him, and all the loyal supporters who helped him risked their lives.

This is the King's own account of what happened, which he dictated to Samuel Pepys in 1680. For the sake of clarity, it has been shortened a little, and some changes have been made in the seventeenth-century spelling and grammar.

After the battle was absolutely lost, I began to think of the best way of saving myself; and the first thought that came into my head was to get to London, if I possibly could, before the news of our defeat could get there. It was near dark, and I asked some of my followers, especially my Lord Wilmot, their opinions of the best way for me to escape. It was impossible, I thought, to get back into Scotland. We had such a number of beaten men with us that I tried as soon as ever it was dark, to get away from them; but, although I had not been able to get them to stand by me against the enemy, I found I could not get rid of them now I had a mind to it.

At last, we got together about sixty gentlemen and officers, and went along northward towards Scotland. We slipped away off the highroad, and kept on the right hand of it, letting all the beaten men go along the road.

We went that night about twenty miles, to a place called Whiteladies, where we stopped just as it was beginning to be day, and got some little refreshment of bread and cheese. And just as we arrived there, a countryman came in and told us that there were three thousand of our horse hard by upon the heath, all in disorder. Some of the people with me were very anxious that I should join these horse and try to go to Scotland with them. But I thought that was absolutely impossible, because

I knew very well that the country would all rise upon us, and that men who had deserted me when they were in good order would never stand to me when they had been beaten.

This made me resolve to disguise myself, and try to get a-foot to London in a countryman's clothes. At the house of White-ladies I took a pair of ordinary grey cloth breeches, a leathern doublet and a green jerkin. I also cut my hair very short, and flung my clothes into a privy-house, that nobody might see that anybody had been stripping themselves. I told nobody of my resolution to go to London except my Lord Wilmot: indeed they all begged me not to tell them what I intended to do, because they did not know what they might be forced to con-fess. So all the persons of quality and officers who were with me, except my Lord Wilmot, resolved to go and join with the three thousand disordered horse, thinking to get away with them to Scotland. But, as I expected, they had not marched six miles before they were all routed by a single troop of horse, which showed that my opinion was right in not sticking to men who had already run away.

As soon as I was disguised I took with me a country-fellow, whose name was Richard Penderell. He was a Roman Catholic, and I chose to trust them, because I knew they had hiding holes for priests, that I thought I might make use of in case of need.

On the morning after the battle, when it was broad day, I left the house with this country-fellow, and set myself at the edge of a great wood, near a highway, the better to see who came after us, and whether they made any search after the runaways. In this wood I stayed all day, without meat or drink. I soon saw a troop of horse coming by, but by great good fortune it rained all the time, which hindered them, I believe, from coming into the wood to search for men that might be fled there. As I lay in the wood, my mind changed, and I decided upon another way of making my escape: to get over the River Severn into Wales, and so to get either to Swan-sea or some other of the sea towns that I knew had commerce with France, where I might take ship. This was a way I thought none would suspect my taking; and I remember several honest gentlemen that I knew in Wales.

So that night, as soon as it was dark, Richard Penderell and I took our journey on foot towards the Severn, intending to pass over a ferry. But as we were going in the night, about twelve or one o'clock, we came by a mill when I heard some people talking. Richard Penderell desired me not to answer if anybody should ask any questions, because I had not the accent of the country. Just as we came to the mill, we could see the miller sitting at the mill door. It was a very dark night, and he was in white clothes. He called out, 'Who goes there?' Upon which Richard Penderell answered, 'Neighbours going home', or some such like words. Whereupon the miller cried out, 'If you be neighbours, stand, or I will knock you down.' As we believed there was company in the house, Richard Penderell bade me follow him close: and he ran to a gate that went up a dirty lane, up a hill. Opening the gate, the miller cried out, 'Rogues! Rogues!' And some men came out of the mill after us, which I believed were soldiers. So we fell a-running, both of us, up the lane as long as we could run. It was very deep and very dirty, and at last I bade him leap over the hedge and lie still to hear if anybody followed us. This we did, and continued lying down upon the ground about half an hour, when, hearing nobody come, we continued on our way to the village above the Severn. The fellow told me there was an honest gentleman, one Mr Woolfe, that lived in the town, and I might go to his house with safety for he had hiding holes for priests. But I would not go in until I knew a little of his mind, whether he would receive so dangerous a guest as me. I therefore stayed in a field, under a hedge, by a great tree, and commanded Richard Penderell not to say it was I, but only to ask Mr Woolfe whether he would receive an English gentleman, a person of quality, to hide him the next day until we could travel again by night – for I only dared to move by night.

When the country-fellow told Mr Woolfe that it was a gentleman who had escaped from the battle of Worcester, Mr Woolfe said it was so dangerous to harbour anybody that he would not risk his neck for any man unless it was the King himself. Upon which, Richard Penderell, very indiscreetly, and without any leave, told him that it was I. Mr Woolfe replied that he was ready to risk all he had in the world to help me. Richard Penderell came and told me what he had done. I was a little troubled, but there was no remedy, the day was just coming on, and I must either venture this or run some greater danger.

So I went into the house by a back way, where I found Mr Woolfe, an old gentleman. He told me he was very sorry to see me there, because there were two companies of the militia in the town, who kept a guard at the ferry and examined everybody that came that way. He dared not put me into any of the hiding holes of his house, because they had already been discovered, and if the soldiers came to search the house they would certainly look first in the holes. So after he had given us some cold meat, I went, without making any bustle in the house, and lay in his barn all the next day behind his corn and hay. Towards evening, Mr Woolfe and his son brought us meat into the barn, and we discussed whether we might safely get over the Severn into Wales. They advised me by no means to adventure upon it, because of the strict guards that were kept all along the river. I therefore resolved to go the same way back again that night to Penderell's house and try again to go for London.

So we set out as soon as it was dark. But as we came by the mill again, we had no mind to be questioned a second time there. I asked Richard Penderell whether he could swim or no, and how deep the stream was. He told me it was a scurvy river, not easy to pass, and that he could not swim. I told him I would undertake to take him over. We went over some meadows to the riverside, and since I could swim I entered the river first, to see whether I could myself go over. I found it was only a little above my middle, and taking Richard Penderell by the hand I helped him over.

Towards morning, we came to the house of one of Penderell's brothers. There was one Major Careless in the house, whom I knew, for he had been a Major in our army and had made his escape thither. He told me it would be very dangerous for me either to stay in that house, or to go into the wood again. He knew only one way how to pass the next day, and that was to get up into a great oak, where we might see round about us; for the enemy would certainly search at the wood for people that had made their escape. I approved of his proposition, and he and I went, taking with us some victuals for the whole day, bread, cheese, small beer and nothing else, and got up into a great oak, which had been lopped some three or four years before and had grown out again very bushy and thick, so that it could not be seen through. Here we stayed all the day. While we were in the tree, we saw soldiers going up and down in the thicket of the wood, searching for persons escaped. We saw them now and then, peeping out of the wood.

Meantime, Penderell's brother brought me word that my Lord Wilmot was at the house of a very honest gentleman, Mr Whitgrave, that there was a very secure hiding hole in Mr Whitgrave's house, and that he desired me to come there to him.

That night Richard Penderell and I went to Mr Whitgrave's, about six or seven miles off. Here I spoke with my Lord Wilmot, and sent him away to Colonel Lane's, about five or six miles off, to see what means could be found for my escaping towards London. Colonel Lane told my Lord, after some consultation, that he had a sister who had a very good excuse to go towards Bristol, to a cousin of hers who lived near the city. She might take me there as her serving man, and from Bristol I might find shipping to get out of England.

So the next night I went away to Colonel Lane's, where I changed my clothes into a little better habit, like a serving man, being a kind of grey cloth suit. The next day Mrs Lane and I took our journey towards Bristol, she riding pillion behind me. But we had not gone two hours on our way but the mare I rode on cast a shoe; so we were forced to ride to get another shoe at a scattering village. And as I was holding my horse's foot, I asked the smith what news? He told me there was no news that he knew of since the good news of the beating of the rogues the Scots. I asked him whether there was none of the English taken, that joined with the Scots. He answered that he had not yet heard that the rogue Charles Stuart was taken; some of the others, he said, were taken, but not Charles Stuart. I told him that if that rogue were taken he deserved to be hanged, more than all the rest, for bringing in the Scots. Upon which he said that I spoke like an honest man, and so we parted.

As soon as ever we came to her cousin's house, Mrs Lane called the butler of the house, a very honest fellow whose name was Pope, and she bade him to take care of William Jackson (for that was my name) as having been lately sick of an ague, whereof she said I was still weak and not quite recovered. And the truth is, my fatigues and want of meat had indeed made me look a little pale. Pope had been a trooper in the King my father's army; but I was not to be known in that house for anything but Mrs Lane's servant. Pope took great care of me that night. I did not eat with the servants, as I otherwise should have done, upon account of my not being well.

The next morning I arose pretty early, having a very good stomach, and went to the buttery hatch to get my breakfast; where I found Pope and two or three other men in the room, and we all fell to eating bread and butter, to which he gave us very good ale and sack. A country-fellow sat just by me, who gave so particular an account of the battle of Worcester that I concluded that he must be one of Cromwell's soldiers. I asked him how he came to give so good an account of the battle. He told me he was in the King's regiment. I asked him what kind of a man I was. To which he answered by describing exactly both my clothes and my horse; and then looking at me, he told me that the King was at least three fingers taller than I. I made what haste I could out of the buttery, for fear he should know me. I was more afraid when I knew he was one of our own soldiers, than when I took him for one of the enemies.

Pope and I went into the hall, and just as we came into it the lady of the house was coming through it. I plucked off my hat, and stood with my hat in my hand as she passed by. Pope looked very earnestly in my face. But I took no notice of it, but put on my hat again and went away, walking out of the house into the field.

When I had been out half an hour, I came back and went up to the chamber where I lay; and just as I came thither, a cousin of Mrs Lane came to me and, in a little trouble, said, 'What shall I do? I am afraid Pope knows you, for he says very positively to me that it is you, but I have denied it.' I asked him whether Pope was a very honest man or no. He answered that he knew him to be so honest a fellow that he durst trust him with his life, as having been always on our side. I thought it better to trust him than go away leaving him in doubt; and thereupon sent for Pope and told him that I was very glad to meet him there, and would trust him with my life as an old acquaintance. He asked me what I intended to do. 'For,' says he, 'I am extremely happy I know you, for otherways you might run great danger in this house. For though my Master and mistress are good people, yet there are one or two in it at this time that are very great rogues; and I think I can be useful to you in anything you will command me.' Upon which I told him my design of getting a ship, if possible, at Bristol; and bade him go that very day immediately to Bristol, to see if there were any ships going either to Spain or France, that I might get a passage away in.

Pope went to Bristol to inquire for a ship, but could hear of none ready to depart beyond sea sooner than within a month, which was too long for me to stay thereabout. So I discussed afresh with my Lord Wilmot and Pope what was to be done. And Pope told me that there lived in that country, upon the edge of Somerset, Frank Windham, the Knight Marshal's brother. He was my old acquaintance, and a very honest man, and so I resolved to go to his house.

But the night before we were to go away, we had a misfortune that might have done us much harm; for Mrs Norton, who was big with child, fell into labour, and miscarried of a dead child, and was very ill; so that we could not tell how in the world to find an excuse for Mrs Lane to leave her cousin in that condition. Yet it was not safe to stay longer there, where there were so many disaffected idle people.

At length, I thought the best way was to counterfeit a letter from her father's house, old Mr Lane's, to tell her that her father was extremely ill, and to command her to come to him immediately, for fear that she should not otherwise find him alive. Pope delivered this letter so well, while they were all at supper, and Mrs Lane played her part so dexterously, that all believed old Mr Lane to be indeed in great danger, and gave his daughter the excuse to go away with me the very next morning early.

Accordingly the next morning we went to Frank Windham's house, which was at Trent near Sherborne. I had appointed my Lord Wilmot to meet me there. I could never get him to put on any disguise, he saying that he should look frightfully in it. And therefore I took care not to keep him with me, but sent him a little before, or left him to come after me.

When we came to Trent, my Lord Wilmot and I consulted with Frank Windham whether he had any acquaintances at any sea-town upon the coast of Dorset or Devonshire. Upon this, he went himself to Lyme, and spoke with a merchant there, to hire a ship for my transportation, being forced to acquaint him that it was I that was to be carried out. The merchant undertook it, and accordingly hired a vessel for France, appointing a day for my coming to Lyme to embark. We set out from Trent, and to disguise our journey better I rode before a cousin of Frank Windham's, one Mrs Juliana Coningsby, still going by the name of William Jackson. We were directed by the merchant to a little village hard by Lyme, named Charmouth. The vessel was to come out of the harbour at Lyme, and come to a little creek that was just by this village and to send their boat ashore to take us in and to carry us over to France, the wind being then very good at north.

So we sat up that night, expecting the ship to come out, but she failed us. I sent Frank Windham's servant, and my Lord Wilmot, to Lyme the next morning, to know the reason of it. But we were much troubled how to pass away our time the next day, till we could have an answer. At last we resolved to go to a place called Bridport, about four miles from Lyme, and there stay till my Lord Wilmot should bring us news whether the vessel could be had the next night or no, and the reason for her last night's failure.

So Frank Windham, and Mrs Coningsby and I, went in the morning on horseback away to Bridport; and just as we came into the town, I could see the streets full of redcoats, Cromwell's soldiers, at which Frank Windham was very much startled, and asked me what I would do. I told him we must go impudently into the best inn in the town and take a chamber there, as the only thing to be done; because we should otherways miss my Lord Wilmot. So we rode directly into the best inn of the place, and found the yard full of soldiers. I alighted, and taking the horses thought it the best way to go blundering in among them, and lead them through the middle of the soldiers into the stable, which I did; and they were very angry with me for my rudeness.

As soon as I came into the stable I took the bridle off the horses, and called the hostler to me to help me, and to give the horses some oats. And as the hostler was helping me to feed the horses, 'Sure, sir,' he says, 'I know your face?' Which was no very pleasant question to me. But I thought the best way was to ask him where he had lived. He told me that he was but newly come thither; that he was born in Exeter, and had been hostler in an inn there, hard by one Mr Potter's, a merchant, in whose house I had lain in the time of war. So I thought it best to give the fellow no further occasion of thinking where he had seen me, for fear he should guess right at last. Therefore I told him, 'Friend, certainly you have seen me then at Mr Potter's, for I served him a good while, above a year.' 'Oh!' says he, 'then I remember you a boy there.' With that, he was put off from thinking any more on it; but desired that we might drink a pot of beer together. This I excused by saying that I must go wait on my master, and get his dinner ready for him. But I told him that my master was going for London, and would return about three weeks hence, and then I would not fail to drink a pot with him.

As soon as we had dined, my Lord Wilmot came into the town from Lyme, but went to another inn. Upon this, we rode out of town, as if we had gone upon the road towards London; and when we were got two miles off, my Lord Wilmot overtook us and told us that he believed the ship might be ready next night. I sent in Frank Windham's servant to ask the merchant whether the ship would be ready. But the master of the ship, doubting that it was some dangerous employment that he was hired upon, absolutely refused the merchant, and would not carry us over. So we were forced to go back again to Frank Windham's house at Trent, where we might be in some safety till we had hired another ship.

One day, during my stay at Trent, I heard the bells ring (the church being hard by Frank Windham's house), and seeing a company got together in the churchyard, I sent down the maid of the house, who knew me, to inquire what the matter was. Returning she came up and told me that there was a rogue, a trooper come out of Cromwell's army, that was telling the people that he had killed me, and that the buff coat he was wearing was mine. Upon which, most of the village being fanatics, they were ringing the bells and making a bonfire for joy of it.

As soon as we came to Frank Windham's, I went away to Colonel Robin Philips, who lived then at Salisbury, to see what he could do for the getting me a ship. He undertook it very willingly, and got one at Southampton, but by misfortune she was pressed to transport Cromwell's soldiers to Jersey, by which she failed us also.

Upon this, I sent further into Sussex, where Robin Philips knew one Colonel Gunter, to see whether he could hire a ship anywhere upon that coast. I did not think it convenient for me to stay much longer at Frank Windham's, where I had been in all about a fortnight, and was become known to very many; so I went directly away to a widow gentlewoman's house, one Mrs Hyde, some four miles from Salisbury. I came into the house just as it was almost dark, with Robin Philips only, not intending at first to make myself known. But just as I alighted at the door Mrs Hyde knew me, though she had never seen me but once in her life, and that was with the King my father in the army, when we marched by Salisbury some years before, in the time of the war. But she being a discreet woman took no notice of me at that time. I passed only for a friend of Robin Philips's.

While we were at supper, I observed Mrs Hyde and her brother Frederick to look a little earnestly at me, which led me to believe they might know me. But I was not at all startled at it, since it had been my purpose to let her know who I was.

After supper she came to me, and I discovered myself to her; and she told me she had a very safe place to hide me in, till we knew whether our ship was ready or no. But she said it was not safe for her to trust anybody but herself and her sister; and she therefore advised me to take my horse next morning and make as if I quitted the house, and return about night. Then she would arrange that all her servants, and everybody but herself and her sister, should be out of the house.

So Robin Philips and I took our horses, and went as far as Stonehenge, and there we stayed looking upon the stones for some time; and we returned back again to Mrs Hyde's house about the hour she appointed. Then I went up into the hiding hole, which was very convenient and safe, and stayed there all alone four or five days.

After those four or five days, Robin Philips came to the house, and told me that a ship was ready for me at Shoreham, provided by Colonel Gunter. At two o'clock in the morning, I went out of the house by the back way, and with Robin Philips I met Colonel Gunter and my Lord Wilmot together, some fourteen or fifteen miles off, on my own towards Shoreham. We were to lodge that night at a place called Hambleton, seven miles from Portsmouth, because it was too long a journey to go in one day to Shoreham. And here we lay at a house of a brother-in-law of Colonel Gunter's, one Mr Thomas Symons. Here I was not to be known (I being still in the same grey cloth suit as a serving man) though the master of the house was a very honest poor man. While we were at supper, he came in, having been all the day playing the goodfellow at an ale-house in the town, and taking a stool sat with us. Colonel Gunter was talking very feelingly concerning Cromwell and all his party, and Mr Symons went and whispered in his ear, and asked whether I was not some roundheaded rogue's son – for he thought I looked very suspicious. But Colonel Gunter answered for me that he might trust his life in my hands, and he came and took me by the hand, and drank a good glass of beer to me, calling me brother roundhead.

The next day we went to a place four miles off of Shoreham, called Bright-helmstone (Brighton), where we were to meet with the master of the ship. We thought it more convenient for us to meet there than at Shoreham, where the ship was. So when we came to the inn at Bright-helmstone, we met with the merchant who had hired the vessel, in company with her master. Only the merchant knew me, as he had hired her only to carry over a person of quality that was escaped from the battle of Worcester, without naming anybody. I observed that the master of the vessel looked very much upon me. And as soon as we had supped, he called the merchant aside and told him he had not dealt fairly with him; for though he had given him a very good price for carrying over that gentleman, yet he had not been clear with him; for, says he, he is the King, and I very well know him to be so. The merchant denied it, saying that he was mistaken; but the master answered, I know him very well, for he took my ship, together with other fishing vessels at Bright-helmstone in the year 1648 (which was when I commanded the King my father's fleet, and I very kindly let them go again.) But, says he to the merchant, be not troubled at it, for I think I do God and my country good service in preserving the King, and by the grace of God I will venture my life and all for him, and set him safely on shore, if I can, in France. Upon which, the merchant came and told me what had passed between them; and so I found myself under necessity of trusting him. I took no kind of notice of it for the present; but we thought it convenient not to let him go home lest he should ask advice of his wife or anybody else; and so we kept him with us in the inn, and sat up all night drinking beer and taking tobacco with him.

And here I also ran another very great danger, for I felt sure I was known by the master of the inn. As I was standing after supper by the fireside, leaning my hand upon a chair, and all the rest of the company had gone into another room, the master of the inn came in, and fell a talking with me. And looking about, and seeing there was nobody in the room, he upon a sudden kissed my hand that was upon the back of the chair, and said to me 'God bless you wheresoever you go. I do not doubt, before I die, but to be a lord and my wife a lady.' I laughed, and went away into the next room, not desiring then any further discourse with him, there being no remedy against my being known by him. I thought it best for to trust him in that manner, and he proved very honest.

About four o'clock in the morning, myself and the company went towards Shoreham, taking the master of the ship with us on horseback, behind one of our company, and came to the vessel's side, which was not above sixty ton. It was low water, and the vessel was lying dry, so I and my Lord Wilmot got up with a ladder into her, and went and lay down in the little cabin till the tide came to fetch us off.

But I was no sooner got into the ship, and lain down upon the bed, but the master came in to me, fell down upon his knees and kissed my hand; telling me that he knew me very well, and would venture life and all that he had in the world to set me down safe in France.

So about seven o'clock in the morning, at high water, we went out of the port. The master was bound for Poole, loaden with sea-coal, and he did not wish to have it seen from Shoreham that he did not go his intended voyage. Therefore he stood all the day, with a very easy sail, towards the Isle of Wight (only my Lord Wilmot and myself of my company being on board). So about five o'clock in the afternoon, as we were in sight of the Isle of Wight, we stood directly over to the coast of France, the wind then full north.

C. O. JENNINGS

# An Ocean without Shores

When Singapore fell to the Japanese in World War II, thousands
of British troops were captured. Many of them tried to escape, but
it was a very long way to any place of safety.

Captain C. O. Jennings and Bombadier Jackson Hall determined
to sail from the island of Sumatra to Australia, which was 1,590
miles across the Timor Sea. Neither of them had any experience
of sailing, but they found an open seventeen-foot boat named
*Gilca*, and they stocked it with food and set sail.

It was four months before they saw land again. These are
extracts from Jennings's matter-of-fact account of their ordeal.

We started the voyage by securing everything against the possibility of a storm. Hall was very silent and thoughtful, staring
back at the fast receding land, and to cheer him I indulged
in a great deal of light-hearted singing while steering the boat
through a veritable meadow of floating grass. Towards the
evening of May 1st the breeze freshened and sailing was a great
delight. *Gilca* made rapid progress with her new jib sail, and
in a glorious sunset the land faded from our view. We had
learned at school that a red sky at night was a sailor's delight.
It certainly was ours. We prophesied fine weather for the morrow, and lighting our stove, cooked a really good rice meal.
The hours we had spent in the cookhouse on Pulau Dua learning
from the cook had not been wasted, and in our enthusiasm we
were confident of being able to emulate even his cooking of
rice. Watches of three hours on and three off were arranged,
but as neither of us felt tired, we sat and talked far into the
night, sailing dead on our course. We were amused to see a
whole crowd of sea-gulls perched on the outriggers enjoying a
free ride, and jockeying with each other for the best position.
 May 2nd dawned and the breeze became light and tricky,
causing us to tack west then east. Hall became his usual cheerful self, now that land had disappeared and that we had meta-

phorically burned our boats, and he knew there could be no turning back. Handing over the tiller to him, I pulled out a small wood box we called the safe, and which contained the ship's valuables – revolvers, boxes of matches wrapped in oilskin, folded charts, a pair of dividers and a Bible. (The last was the only reading matter we had on board.) With the aid of the dividers and a protractor cut from one of the charts, I prepared a new chart and started a log-book. Estimating our speed at three knots, I plotted the distance for the past nineteen hours, and after comparing the very short line with the great blank space of paper which represented ocean yet to be traversed, I quickly folded the chart and replaced it in the safe, and turned my attention to the practical problem of cooking breakfast and airing the blankets.

We chatted incessantly about many things, but always the talk returned to our immediate well being and, one of the vital problems (in fact, the most vital) being food, we discussed it at great length and agreed that two meals a day would be sufficient as we were more or less lounging and not using our energy in violent exertion. All day contrary winds made steering difficult, and towards evening the wind rose and seas came inboard, compelling us to start bailing with the coconut shells we had provided for the purpose. Dropping the mainsail, we carried on under the jib. The new sail was really proving its worth.

All through the night the gale blew from the south-east, but with the morning it swung round and gave us a fair run. I entered two knots in the log-book for our second day at sea, and pricked the distance off on the chart. Considering we had had a fairly bad night, and feeling we needed a little pampering, I suggested a leg of chicken each had been richly earned. I opened the lid of the tin, when a most awful smell issued therefrom, and we both agreed that the meat had gone bad, or at least that the oil had turned rancid. As we had plenty of other kinds of food the whole of it was dumped over the side without more ado. We recognized the seriousness of such action, but were confident we could re-provision at Christmas Island. The chicken having gone bad caused us to have grave doubts about the saygan (native porridge).There was a great possibility that the desiccated coconut might ferment, so we agreed to eat the N.P. before the rice. This meant cold meals, but there would be hot coffee to finish with.

For hours on end we sat and chatted about our families, homes, work, pleasure, and the kind of things we should really like to do, but always our minds turned back to getting to freedom as quickly as possible, because we were under the impression that after we had been posted missing for six months, the War Office would tell our respective families we were presumed dead. This worried us intensely, as we did not wish to cause them any unnecessary heartburning when here we were just sculling around the Indian Ocean, more or less enjoying ourselves.

Day after day the routine of putting the boat about became monotonous, tacking ten miles east and ten miles west to get a miserable six miles south. The chart had so many jagged lines running across the straight line of the course that it was pure desperation which enabled us to conjure up sufficient optimism to believe we could eventually reach Australia.

Then came storms such as I had never seen before, certainly not from a small boat, and *Gilca* was tossed about like a cork, and needed constant bailing. Fear helped us in getting the boat dry, and the stupid little coconut shells gave place to the tin which had contained the chicken. Using this, it was possible to remove two or three gallons at a time, but it was very much harder work. We got used to being wet through and lying down in a blanket from which the two of us had just wrung the water. Fortunately the storms were nearly always accompanied by deluges of rain, and when this happened we bailed the boat dry, then let it fill again to approximately nine inches in depth, bailed it out once more, and the third filling of rain-water would generally be moderately clear of salt, and with the aid of an enamel mug we would fill the water-tank.

About this time I was unfortunate enough to lose my clothes. Having fastened them securely to a thin grass rope, I flung them into the sea, towing them in our wake. For what seemed hours I kept an eye on them, but a particularly spicy story of Hall's distracted my attention, and when next I remembered my belongings, they had gone and a frayed rope's end was all I retrieved. The boat fairly rocked with my friend's laughter as he twitted me about how easily I could now sunbathe. It made me smile, too, and though it was not unpleasant to be free from the encumbrance of clothes, I felt unsightly and wondered what I should do when we arrived at a civilized place. I wondered even more the following day, when Fate gave me my revenge. I had the laugh at Hall's misfortune in losing his shorts in precisely the same manner, after he had boasted of the knots which secured them to the rope, and which he confidently declared Houdini himself could not escape from. Apparently we had fish following us that knew a thing or two about short-circuiting knots, as again we merely had the frayed rope's end. We began to look worse than I imagine Robinson Crusoe ever looked, particularly when Hall took off his flapping shirt, to save it 'for going ashore in'.

Soreness again began to afflict us, and large red patches appeared between our legs from which the skin peeled off leaving a wet, painful blotch such as one gets by tearing the skin off a blister. The only treatment possible was periodic dabbings with a mixture of fresh and salt water.

About the twentieth day out, while enjoying a spell of reasonably good sailing, we were both surprised to feel something hit the underside of the boat. My first reaction was that the keel had come adrift, so while Hall leaned over the starboard side, I leaned over the other trying to get a glimpse of the makeshift keel. When my companion in a hushed voice said, 'See that, Skip?' 'See what?' I replied. The words were hardly out of my mouth when several huge shapes glided into my line of vision. Sharks! – the first we had seen. We wondered which one had our clothes. From the safety of our boat they were interesting to watch, and both of us agreed that the old wives' tale about there being a death on board ships which a shark followed was all baloney. Here were enough sharks messing about our boat for half a dozen funerals.

While trying to cook our twenty-first evening meal, we suffered a great misfortune; I struck the last match in the box and the wind blew it out, causing Hall to groan loudly. This did not depress me unduly, as I had taken the precaution to hide half a dozen matches in an empty box, and I thought he knew nothing about them. With a superior smile I opened our small safe to produce 'the rabbit from the hat', but my smile turned to an acid grin when, after searching through the pile of boxes, no matches were to be found. The last match was spent, and it then dawned on me that an essential piece of equipment for escapers was a magnifying glass. But it was no use thinking about it. We had exercised great care when lighting matches, but our estimate of three matches a day was obviously very much under the mark, when taking into account the heads that came off whilst we were trying to strike them and the number that broke. But our chief enemy was the wind, which blew out many of them and hindered our progress. To make either tea or coffee was now a slow business entailing a whole night's steeping to produce even the semblance of a taste. Still, we had plenty of food and water, and though conditions could have been better, we did not grouse.

That night a storm broke, so we downed sail and put the sea-anchor over the bows.

Dawn broke to find two very wet and tired men – tired with the constant bailing and wet from breaking seas and torrential rain. Several times our tiny vessel was bailed dry and allowed partially to fill with rain-water so that we could fill the water tank, but a wave would come inboard to spoil the whole lot, setting us frantically bailing again. There came a period when wave upon wave crashed into the boat, and it seemed that we must inevitably founder, as the water came in much faster than we could throw it out. Finally we became so utterly weary as to think we were physically incapable of bailing any more. Yet when the water reached our knees we would start again, with a completely mechanical action that told we had reached the end of our tether, and that desperation was giving way to resignation.

For seven weary days and nights we lay to the sea-anchor while we suffered the vagaries of the storm. It could only be our water-tank which kept us afloat. The tins of food formed small moving islands in the interior of the *Gilca*, while the bed-boards across the thwarts actually floated. This meant that *Gilca* was full of water to within less than eight inches of the true gunwale. To make things more unpleasant, if possible, we were cursed with salt sores once again, but had no time to worry over such comparative trifles. It seemed we were in a storm centre, and the sooner we got away from this place the better. We could not endure this buffeting much longer. The bailing and the constant lack of sleep had completely worn us out. In a great last effort we once more got the boat reasonably dry and lay down, utterly weary, to await the next water invasion.

As the fortieth morning of our voyage broke I opened the safe and produced dividers and chart, plotting the previous day's run, and was able to announce very proudly to my companion, that according to my reckoning, we had just crossed the fourteenth degree of latitude. He asked what that meant in plain English, and I carefully explained about degrees and that North-West Cape was on the twenty-second of these mysterious and imaginary lines, so we had eight more to cross, or approximately 500 miles of ocean to traverse to complete our journey. The jubilation of *Gilca*'s crew knew no bounds; any moment reconnaissance aircraft might come roaring overhead, to say nothing of the possibility of sighting surface craft while crossing the various shipping lanes.

The weather had become much cooler, and what remained of the coconut oil had solidified into a white mass of the same consistency as lard. We would sit at the tiller with blankets wrapped round our naked bodies, and although the temperature caused us some slight discomfort, it was the most obvious and practical indication that we were getting away from the tropics. Chattering about which museum we would put *Gilca* in, I prepared breakfast, and, in celebration of crossing latitude 14 degrees S, I issued an extra spoonful of porridge each, poured on the water and, while waiting for it to swell, we agreed that Perth Museum could have the boat. Handing Hall his plate and spoon, I turned to pick up mine, and before I could start eating he retched violently and spat the stuff into the bilge. I was amazed and asked what was wrong with him. In forthright fashion he told me there was nothing wrong with him, it was the blasted porridge, and I should try it myself. I did, and a moment later Hall had the verification he sought, as I, too was retching and vomiting. The reason was all too clear: the stuff had become impregnated with salt water, but the question was how? Each tin was fitted with a 'press-in' type of lid, making it completely proof against the entry of water. We carefully examined the sides and the bottom. Here we found minute holes with a tell-tale ring of rust round each. How the holes came to be there did not matter: they may have been caused by the sea-water or by the natives. The awful fact remained that all our remaining food was uneatable.

I again produced the chart and carefully studied the distance from Australia, and to my friend in distress put these two questions: 'Do you think we can sail south twenty-five miles a day?' and 'Do you also think you can last twenty days without food?' Hall's answers were typical of the man. To the first question his answer was a plain 'Yes!' To the second, without any hesitation, he replied: 'I'll try, Skipper. A chap once came to my home town and starved for twenty-four days in a glass cage; it was twopence to go in. If he could do it, I reckon I can starve for twenty!' If we could do it, Australia was 'in the bag', and we could make land under our own sail. And there was always that tantalizing hope of being picked up.

We threw the contaminated food overboard and shook hands on 'Australia, or sink'. We redoubled our efforts to reach land within the twenty days by keeping the sail up during squalls and taking just a little more than reasonable risks. We could afford to do this, as without food we were very bad insurance, anyhow. Scanning the horizon, we would often see six or more rainstorms; those to windward we would watch intently, and only drop sail at the very last moment.

Novelists often write 'As the days wore on', but I leave the reader to imagine the agony of each starving minute and hour, when a minute felt like an hour and an hour seemed as long as a whole day. Yet during all this time not once did Hall utter one single grouse, either about food or our desperate situation. I could not have had a better companion. To be sure we talked about food, but only in the abstract sense, that it was as necessary to the human being as fuel was to an internal combustion engine.

We must have looked a queer pair, both naked. The skin on my friend's body had assumed a tender rose-pink, due to exposure. A thick-matted thatch of flaming red hair reached nearly to his shoulders, and with a shaggy beard of the same colour he might easily have been the prototype from which McGlusky sprang. In contrast to Hall, my skin was burned to the colour of a Malay; my hair and beard were of a similar generous length, liberally streaked with grey.

As I have previously mentioned, the only book we had on board was the Bible, and it became our practice at two o'clock each afternoon to read a chapter from the New Testament. Unfortunately my sight had deteriorated to such an extent that I could not see the print, and the reading therefore devolved totally upon Hall. He read clearly and slowly, occasionally putting down the book while we seriously debated upon the various problems that confronted the disciples, being particularly keenly interested in the voyage during which St Paul was wrecked. I had never read the Bible before, and neither, I think, had Hall. Coming to the end of the chapter, he would always finish with 'Here endeth the reading of the Lord's holy word.' The Bible would then be carefully wrapped up and placed in the wood safe along with the charts, and our undivided attention would once more be given to sailing.

June 30th dawned a glorious sunny morning with just the right amount of wind for splendid sailing, provided we had been travelling in the opposite direction. This was our 'deadline' day, the sixty-first at sea and our twentieth without food of any kind. Opening the safe, I took out the chart, which showed we were still two hundred miles from North-West Cape. We felt it strange that no patrolling aircraft had been sighted, and we were not unnaturally disappointed, as we had hoped to be picked up ere now. It was obvious we could not make Australia against the south-west winds, and it was also horribly clear that we could not last much longer without food.

There was only one hope left, and that was to turn and use the wind, making for the eastern tip of Java or the island of Bali, as according to the wind chart the current set in that direction, and ironically it was also the old sailing route to Japan. Conferring on this matter, we agreed, but this time very, very doubtfully, that we would try to hold out without food for another ten days, this being my estimated time to reach Java, where we hoped it might be possible to ship a hundred coconuts and again try for freedom, but next time for Africa. Our motto of 'Australia or sink' had regretfully to be abandoned, and, cursing all aircraft for not picking us up, we put about and laid a course north and east towards the enemy's outstretched arms.

It is difficult to describe our feelings, and to say we felt disappointed would be as inaccurate as to say we were angry. A kind of fatalistic indifference to whatever might happen to us is the description nearest the truth. Sailing in the wrong direction could not be avoided, so there was no reason to chastise ourselves for doing it.

We had lost weight at an alarming rate during the twenty days' fast, and with knee and elbow joints badly swollen we looked pitiable objects. To all intents and purposes our race was run, we were doomed men, and whether we could survive a further ten days' starvation was very problematical. As if to atone for her slow progress on the outward journey, our small craft simply tore through the water, which made us regret not having sailed west from Enggano. The direction of the wind having remained constant we estimated it would have been possible to cross the Indian Ocean within forty days, and our troubles would have been over, added to which we would have achieved something instead of doodling about in the Timor Sea.

Long periods of silence reigned between us. We had said all there was to be said many times over, and it was with pleasurable anticipation that both of us looked forward to something fresh in the daily Bible-reading session. At 2 p.m. Hall produced the Book and read through the chapter, finishing with his usual 'Here endeth the reading of the Lord's holy word.' While wrapping the Bible up and replacing it safely in the wood box, we debated as usual the various points that had arisen during the reading of the chapter, and a little while later he clambered laboriously into the cockpit to relieve me, and I performed the operation in reverse as far as the bed-slats, as it was my intention to snatch forty winks. To give relief to my sore thighs, I commenced the necessary task of making the blanket into a coil similar to that of hawsers which one sees so beautifully coiled and laid out on the decks of warships. The job was nearly completed when a low burring sound forward attracted my attention. I became petrified as I saw beneath the boom a sea-gull hovering with fast-beating wings about a foot above the bowsprit. A quick glance towards my companion told me of his amazement, too. We dared not utter a sound for fear of frightening the bird away. So there was something else in all this wide space besides ourselves! Something other than sharks! It took several seconds before my numbed brain registered the fact that this white feathered object represented food and that I had to do something to get it. My trembling hands crept inch by inch to the chart-box, where I kept my revolver, fortunately oiled and cleaned.

The 'great desire' sat perched on the bowsprit four feet beyond, but still with infinite patience and caution I raised my revolver inch by inch to the firing position and took a 'bead' on the plump portion of the gull's shoulder. Gripping the butt of the weapon with my right hand, my left pinned it to the mast in the hope of eliminating the trembling of my body. Taking a deep breath, I squeezed the trigger gently, and began to think the striker would never work. My eyes began to water; the grey and white target appeared to recede and become indistinct as though I was looking through a pane of untrue glass. The fingers of my left hand were hurting due to the power of the grip in pinning the revolver to the mast. Just when I thought it would be necessary to wipe my eyes and take another breath the weapon fired, and the gull left the bowsprit. My heart seemed to have stopped beating, until through tiny slits my eyes telegraphed the joyful message to my brain that in the shoulder of the bird was a red hole about the size of a sixpence, and the bird was falling into the sea some two feet from the boat. With the report of the revolver, followed by the disappearance of the bird, the tension snapped, and, as silence was no longer necessary, I shouted, 'Jack, get it.' *Gilca* was moving at a decent speed and it was necessary for us to move rapidly, as otherwise the sharks might beat us to it. Hall got the sea-gull in with one of the basket oars we had used on our way over to the islands from Padang. Shaking hands, we chuckled with delight and were half demented over our success, each of us holding and fondling the bird to convince ourselves that this was no dream.

We chatted away like two old women trying to calculate the additional sustenance we would derive from the meat. That ten days' additional starving could certainly be accomplished with such a base to work from was our unanimous decision. A meal of such magnitude seemed unbelievable, and, although terribly hungry, neither of us ate one single piece of flesh until the division had been completed; then Hall put down the knife and said, 'Let's go, Skip.' The serious business of eating had to be given priority; the tiller was lashed, and whether *Gilca* drifted ten miles off her course mattered not one iota. We sat one each side of the water-tank steadily chewing the exquisite raw flesh and looking at each other with smiling eyes, completely happy, and, for the time being, utterly content. This was the first food we had eaten for twenty long days. Six hours later, in the soft light of the evening, we were still chewing bones, chewing them to destruction, in the process of which I broke two teeth off my dentures; but such a thing could not dismay one who felt as I did . . .

This life, if it was life, seemed to consist for me of guiding *Gilca* through the darkness over a sea of darkness, with spells of oblivion in between. Nine such periods, which represented days, passed by, and still no bird arrived. In thirty days we had had three seagulls between us, and now we were more dead than alive. During these nights, I employed the time by putting my arms on the tiller bar, leaning my head on them and keeping my eyes fixed on the compass which I could hardly see. Hope began to fade, and each morning I saw the look of hopelessness on my friend's face. Handing the tiller to him this particular morning, I reminded him that tomorrow we should see land;

it was the only cheerful thing I could think of; and when tomorrow arrived, the tenth day after turning the boat back to Java, our seventieth since setting out from Enggano, I spent an hour very carefully scanning the horizon as I felt sure we must be near land. Turning to Hall I had to admit that no land was visible, but that perhaps it was covered by the haze, though neither of us could see any haze. What excuse could I give? The air was as clear as crystal, there was no land, and we both thought there never would be any for us, and perhaps in another day or so it would not matter.

Two very long days later, I managed to shoot another bird, and needless to say we devoured it ravenously. It was a particularly small gull and merely whetted our appetites, and our craving stomachs caused us to look at our boots with envy. Why should not we eat them? Hungry as I was, I remembered my mother telling me a story as a child of one of our relations who was wrecked on a desert island. He ate his boots, was finally rescued, only to die shortly after with cancer on the tongue. This story I now related to Hall, and it was sufficient to make us leave our boots alone and turn our attention to a shark which was following the boat. If we could get it to come sufficiently close to us, there was a possibility of shooting it. This would provide our bare cupboard with food for days. The sail was lowered and the shark gained on us, but the big fish never came nearer than twenty yards. So I fired, hoping for a lucky hit, but it did not seem to be affected. It was only after the third shot that it turned away and left us. We were convinced it had been hit and very badly wounded, so the sea-anchor rope was put over in the hope that within an hour or so the fish would come floating, belly up, to the surface. I remember having read in some book or other that dead sharks did this kind of thing, but it may have been whales or crocodiles.

After searching the surrounding water for some three hours in the hope that the shark would turn up, we were forced to the conclusion that it was not dead, and reluctantly got under way again. While Hall steered, I cleaned the revolver and prepared to load it ready for use. The ammunition was kept in our respective haversacks, and great was our disappointment when, turning them both out, the combined result was one round – the last round.

That night was one of the most horrible we experienced; one moment we could have cried with joy, and the next we literally cried with grief and despair. It was a Sunday evening, and the light was just beginning to fade when another of our white and grey winged saviours came out of the sky. The bird seemed wary, and circled round the boat several times, making us dreadfully afraid it was not going to land, and with the saliva forming in our mouths, we lay absolutely motionless hoping and waiting. It was getting rapidly darker when the bird finally dropped on the bowsprit, and I dared not waste any time in drawing a 'bead' on it or the light would beat me, and the gull kept rising a foot or so as though it realized that our boat was not a healthy spot. Immediately before the striker pin came against the firing cap of our last round, the bird spread its wings; but before it could leave the bowsprit, the tell-tale dark round hole appeared in its shoulder. It fell into the sea, dead, some five feet from *Gilca*, and though we touched it with the oars we could not draw it in. The current appeared to be taking it away from us very rapidly, so we put the boat about in an endeavour to pick it up. For an hour or more we tacked about for that floating bunch of feathers which meant so much to us, but in the darkness that was now night, the quest was hopeless and we put the boat back on her course. This, so far, seemed to be our blackest day; we had had food within our grasp and missed it. Somewhere out there on the water floated a dead sea-gull. That night we cried ourselves to sleep, having tried to console each other that we really did not want that bird anyhow; but what worried me most was the fact that we had no more ammunition.

During the early hours I awakened and looked up at the sky. The darkness of night at sea always amazed me as it was possible to see anything in the boat at any hour of the night. My eyes travelled round and came to rest on the mast, which seemed to have become longer. I began to wonder if I were still asleep, as on the top reposed a sea-gull, or a ghost of one, and daring to look away, I lowered my eyes to Hall's recumbent figure and touched him ever so lightly. He awakened. I whispered, asking him to look on top of the mast. We rolled back our blankets like automatons, rose together, and with a tap on my chest and a quick effort at pantomime, I indicated that I, being much the lighter, would climb up the mast. Hall nodded and imitated pushing me up to let me know he understood. We felt we dare not talk. The boat was swaying, and I had some little difficulty in getting started with the climbing. Standing on the thwart together, I stretched as high as I could and gripped the mast, while Hall pushed like a Trojan. Then near the top I stretched out an arm, and measuring the last few inches, put an additional spurt into my climbing and with fingers extended gripped the bird's legs. I thought nothing could have made me release the grip I had on that bird; though it pecked my hand unmercifully, they were mere kisses to me. The bird created an awful din, and delirious with happiness I tried to shout the joyful news to my friend that I had got it, as though he did not know. He let my feet go, and I came hurtling down the mast with a searing pain down the middle of my naked body, due to leaving a considerable amount of skin on it; and I was glad Hall took the gull from me before I was half-way down, otherwise I might have let the bird go, the pain was so intense. We had got another meal, and, making our gladsome way to the tiller cockpit, the bird's head was cut off and our usual procedure gone through. The rest of that night was spent in an orgy of feeding. It was a regular blood bath, and we were happy again, particularly because we had proved that seagulls could be caught by hand provided the hunter was not visible to the bird . . .

On August 1st, Bank Holiday, we fortunately caught an adult sea-gull and a small black bird. So everything was rosy once more, except that the jack-knife was lost; Hall had gathered up the feathers and heaved them over the side, both of us being completely ignorant of the fact that the knife had also gone. Whilst eating our supper we talked about Scarborough, Blackpool and the different fairs that we supposed would be in full swing at home, and the good times we had previously and would again if ever we got out of this mess.

The next day dawned with hardly a ripple on the ocean and not a breath of wind to fill the slatting sail. The sun climbed the heavens while we searched vainly for sight of land or a bird, but never again did a sea-gull land on our boat, nor did we even see one. In all, we had eaten some sixty of these sea birds, and to them we undoubtedly owe our lives. We talked of gulls, and in particular of the statue erected to them in Utah for the work they did in clearing a swarm of locusts from the Mormons' crops. We also discussed Captain Bligh quite a bit and felt sure we had now been at sea nearly as long as he had. little did we realize that the *Bounty's* men had made their historic journey in only forty-eight days.

Day after day that same hateful sea still remained. We began to wonder whether or not the doldrums had moved from the Pacific to the Indian Ocean and wished a storm would spring up to relieve the monotony, but there seemed little hope of that. Having talked about everything, we relapsed into silence, just watching, waiting and starving. To shut out the brassy glare of the sun's reflected light we spent most of this period lying down with a corner of the blanket over our eyes. This period of total abstinence from food seemed very much worse than the previous ones. It was obvious we had at last reached the breaking point, and quiet sobs from the direction of Hall's blanket brought me out of my stupor to give him a few words of encouragement, to which he replied, 'Leave me alone, Skipper; I'm in one of my moods again; it will soon pass off.' Poor devil, his young and large body must have craved for food even more than mine, and heaven knows I would have given anything for a good square meal. During all this time our Bible-reading continued, and we looked forward to the daily chapter with very real pleasure. Reading the New Testament by chapters seemed rather like seeing a serial film, leaving the hero hanging over a precipice with the caption, 'What happens to him? See next week's instalment.' We felt the same about Paul when he was cast into prison. 'Would he make the grade?' Things looked very black against us, too – should we make it?

The seventh consecutive day of starvation came, and at 2 p.m. Hall dragged the tattered, water-soaked Bible from his haversack and began to read. I was much interested, for there was something about food; and, peculiarly, there were tables full of it with people standing by just to hand one any delicacy one desired. Then someone said, 'Here endeth the reading of the Lord's holy word.' It seemed most strange; the viands vanished and I wondered what the Lord's holy word had to do with all that food that was about to be given to me. Lifting my head from the blanket, I saw Hall's unlovely face and realized I had been dreaming.

I spent the whole morning looking for land, seated up forward – if one can get forward in a boat seventeen feet long; at about 11.30 Hall came clambering to where I was sitting, and with parted lips and shining eyes, excitement written all over his face, he leaned over me and in a tense whisper said, 'Skipper, at the back of the boat is a tortoise, like one of those things you have in the garden.' Realizing he meant a turtle, I got off the thwart and quietly, and as quickly as possible, we went aft, four very bony legs clambering over beds and into the tiller cockpit. And as though the thing was imperceptible to anyone but himself, Hall was pointing at a turtle within a yard of the rudder, saying in a soft voice, 'It's there, Skip; it's there!' It was quite a homely-looking creature, but not knowing how turtles reacted to human beings, I was afraid it might dive beyond our reach if I spoke aloud, so I contented myself with a quiet 'O.K., Jack; let's get it,' meanwhile wondering what damage the thing might do to our hands with its parrot-like beak. Curiosity did not deter us, Hall taking the right-hand and I the left-hand flipper or the claw, or whatever the foreleg of a turtle is called. In two shakes an eighteen-inch turtle was lying on its back in the bilge, as, in accordance with more theoretical knowledge I had absorbed, this was the orthodox manner in which turtles were killed; and while moistening our lips at the thought of food, we waited for it to die. After five long minutes the turtle seemed as lively as ever, and as we could not wait any longer condemned it to execution. With one blow of the axe Hall beheaded it, and then began chopping out the belly skin with the axe. It was then that we found the jack-knife missing.

On August 9th the turtle was finished with the exception of the shell, and we cast around for more 'eats'. The hard belly-skin or shell of the turtle was chopped up; we sucked pieces of it, and tried chewing it, but found it impossible to swallow. A fin cutting the water near *Gilca* set us wondering if it would not be possible to get the shark into the boat. For days it had circled us, and at times had been so near that we could have leaned over the gunwale and touched it. Had we had any ammunition, it would have been a simple matter to have replenished our larder. It appeared half-grown, about four feet long, and would provide us with food for many days if only we could catch it. Waving a piece of cloth about in the water, we finally enticed it to come near enough for me to grab one of its lateral fins and Hall the other, whilst with his other hand my companion picked up the axe and chopped at the shark's back, hoping to injure its spine. The blade cut deeply into the flesh, leaving a light-grey wound. It must have become annoyed, as it commenced lashing its tail. Realizing one good lash would tear the thing from our grasp, I took the axe from Hall and aimed a blow at its head with all the strength I possessed, hoping to puncture the brain. This last effort caused it to leap partly out of the sea, and crashing into the rudder, smashed it and tore free from our grasp. Stretching outboard, I aimed a final blow at its disappearing head and, due to my hands being wet, the shaft slipped through my fingers and the axe was lost. Knife gone, axe gone. Here was a pretty kettle of fish – and yet no fish. Fortunately we had a hammer, and with it completed repairs to the rudder for the third time. The shark-hunt had been very exciting, and at one stage of the fight we all but pulled it into the boat. Had Hall aimed his original blows at the monster's head in the first instance, instead of wasting his strength in stretching to try to injure its spine, we might have captured it. After this episode we never saw another shark.

A favourable wind sprang up, and for two days *Gilca* made good headway along her north-eastern course, but still no land was to be seen. We were most definitely not going round in circles. The chart showed that we had entirely crossed Java and were approaching the island of Ambon. The whole thing had become ridiculous, and I stopped plotting and contented myself by studying the wind chart and currents. We were somewhere on that patch of blue – but where? And how far from land? We had no food, but plenty of rusty-coloured water. How long could one hold out on water alone? There could be no answer. Again silence reigned between us and we sat just staring, steering and hoping, while *Gilca* sailed lazily onward across a sea of burnishing gold. The end seemed near, and, in contrast to a fevered body, it seemed that an ice-cold calculator had replaced my brain, and this new contraption was detached and placed just out of reach above my head. Nothing mattered; I was above such mundane things as eating; I was incapable of feeling. It seemed as if my body was no thicker than a piece of cardboard, furnished with glazed movable eyes imparting to my mind a flat vision. Only during times of sleep would the horrible bogy of food obtrude, and my trembling hands would reach towards the dream food, when the fantasy of tormenting hell would recede beyond my grasp, leaving me in an agony of despair; and with pleading words and faltering dream-steps I would follow, until physical requirements woke me, and my friendly kindly calculator would again take charge of the wasted thing that was me, reiterating for the thousandth time that food did not matter, that there was no need to worry about anything as there was no tomorrow, no yesterday and really no today. And so I would sit and stare at my bony legs or at the golden sea, and in moments of weakness at the distant horizon whence would come – the land. Once while looking over the side watching beautiful fish gliding beneath the boat, I noticed several barnacles on the water-line. Here was a discovery of far more moment to us than a Klondyke or a Kimberley. We reached down into the water and cleared as many barnacles as we could; about half a mugful. They looked rather like whelks, and as we pulled them off the boat-side a blob of grey camouflage paint came with them. Devouring them, we crunched shells and paint, the while likening them to oysters owing to their pleasant taste. They proved to be most sustaining though we did wonder what the crunched-up shells would do to our intestines. It was perhaps this thought, coupled with logic and a streak of caution, that enabled us to refrain from immediately clearing the boat of barnacles and eating the lot there and then. Each day we removed a mugful, and a week passed before the last of the limpets fouling *Gilca's* bottom had gone. This was the only food we had been able to obtain, but both Hall and I suffered no ill-effects other than violent diarrhoea, which was probably caused by the paint.

The good weather again deserted us. We were beset by violent storms. We suffered the tortures of the damned in constant bailing, and more maddening bailing. Yet the boat became dangerously full of water as we had not now the energy to combat the inflow due to torrential rain and heavy seas; also the coldness of the rain affected us much more keenly now. The storm gave us more fresh water and two small flying fish, and as it blew itself out we were overjoyed to find a small bunch of seaweed about the size of a wire scrubber and with the same springy texture; the important thing was that it was eatable. As the days rolled by seaweed became more plentiful and small boughs began to float past. All these things we pulled into the boat, and Hall developed a great liking for boughs, whilst I remained partial to seaweed. When I caught boughs I handed them over to him, and he reciprocated with seaweed.

August 1942, was drawing to its close, and we had now been at sea 123 days. It almost seemed that land was a myth, that this really was an ocean without shores, and that the whole of our lives had been lived together in this little boat sailing everywhere but nowhere. Neither did there appear to be any change except fine weather and stormy weather; always there was the sea and hunger. We had turned *Gilca* round on the sixty-first day, hoping to reach the eastern end of Java in ten days. Then came the twentieth, the thirtieth, fortieth, fiftieth, sixtieth day. Would this never end? By all the normal laws and theories of man we should have been dead long ago. Though we were weak and emaciated, the spark of life still burned within us and the hope of making the grade we scarcely once doubted.

Early the next morning we watched the sun's golden rays creeping steadily up behind a cloud, and lo! the cloud became a mountain, towering thousands of feet into an azure sky. We remained staring; spellbound! We were satisfied just to look at it and drink our fill of the one thing we had craved for so long. Land!

They were back in Sumatra where they had started. *Gilca* was wrecked when they landed in the surf, and a few hours later, after all they had suffered, they were captured by the Japanese.

– from *An Ocean Without Shores*

# Escape from the Jungle

Through most of the first half of the nineteenth century, explorers were trying to find a route to cut a canal across the isthmus of Panama. In 1850, an Irishman named Dr Cullen claimed he had found a place where he could walk across in two or three days. An expedition of the United States Navy was sent to confirm this route – twenty-seven men commanded by Lieutenant I. G. Strain. From Cullen's description, they expected an easy walk. But after ten days in the jungle they were lost, and they made a fatal mistake: they started to follow the river which they thought led straight to the Gulf of Darien on the Pacific Coast. But it was the wrong river, and it led in fact by a tortuous course over two hundred miles.

Strain's men were weak with hunger, and some could hardly move. He decided to leave most of them, and press on down the river with only three companions to try to find help.

Behind the old fashioned English of this report is an extraordinary tale of endurance and escape in tropical jungle.

On February 14th, at earliest dawn, they were afoot. Having obtained no food the day before, there was no delay in cooking and eating. They were soon forced from the river by the undergrowth, and after a march of about two hours, found themselves in a dense thicket, where it was necessary to cut every foot of the way for some two hundred yards. During the time they occupied in making this distance they rarely if ever touched the earth, so matted and close were the standing and fallen branches and bushes. It was painful work, and not without danger; but they cut and floundered through. Emerging into the more open forest, they found themselves in an almost impassable swamp. Struggling through this as they best could, they saw a large body of water, and Strain, in attempting to approach it, became so effectually bogged, that it was with great difficulty he extricated himself. The order to countermarch was then given, and after incredible labour they reached the river about noon, and at a point only about 200 yards below the camp from which they had set out some seven hours before. This was disheartening, but they pushed on for two hours longer when they halted for an hour's rest.

Strain now felt quite discouraged; for, at this rate, the party would perish before it could get through. He determined, therefore, to try a raft, and finding on the beach some driftwood sufficiently dry to float, he halted at four o'clock and commenced collecting timbers, cutting cross-pieces, and getting vines for lashings. This was slow work, as they had nothing with which to cut the hard logs – that were in some cases imbedded in the earth – except the machete (a sort of cutlass of good steel and highly tempered). Still, by working hard, they had by dark collected enough logs to float two or three men. They then began to look around for some food, not having tasted a mouthful since the night previous to leaving the main body, two days before. Having obtained a few acid nuts, they made a fire, spread their blankets, and were soon fast asleep on a hard clay bank, with a brilliant full moon shining down upon them.

At daylight they were hard at work upon the raft, and by ten o'clock had logs enough lashed together to support two persons. Wilson and Strain then got upon it, and pushing off, slowly floated down the river; while Mr Avery and Golden followed along the bank.

At noon another large log was secured and lashed to the raft with strips of canvas torn from Strain's haversack, and the whole party embarked. But the weight was too heavy, and the crazy structure sank until the water was knee-deep above it. They, however, kept on, but in a short time struck a rapid current which swept them upon a sunken snag. In a moment the logs parted and one broke entirely loose. All was consternation, when Strain cried, 'Silence!' and sitting down on one log, threw either leg over those each side and kept them together. For a few minutes there was great danger of losing all their arms, and even their lives; and nothing but the presence of mind and coolness of every man saved the raft from entire destruction and in deep water, while, owing to the debility and the weight of their accoutrements, swimming was out of the question.

Landing below, where the current was not so strong, they repaired the raft, and floated sluggishly on till nearly sunset, when they struck upon a shoal. Unable to force the raft over this, they were compelled to take it to pieces and float it down, log by log, to a shelving clay beach, where they could reconstruct it. While getting the raft over they discovered a species of clams – one hundred and twenty of which made quite a supper, after their hard day's work. While sitting on the bank they saw a shark, some five feet long, attempting to swim over the shoal; but all attempts to get his body for food proved abortive.

The next day, by nine o'clock, the raft was repaired, and the four again embarked; Strain with nothing on but a shirt – barelegged, sat exposed to the full rays of a tropical sun, and with the rest not much better protected, drifted lazily down the sluggish, tortuous current. At noon, however, they struck another snag. While working hard to extricate themselves, a heavy rain shower came up, which drenched them thoroughly. Soon after another snag was struck, which caused a delay of two hours. Near sunset they came upon a shoal, and swinging off met a swift current, and were dragged by its force under some overhanging branches, which swept Mr Avery and Golden off into deep water, while Strain, with Wilson, whose leg was nearly broken, hung on, and were carried upon a snag in deep water. In endeavouring to cut loose, they lost a machete. But Golden, finding his leg not broken, plunged to the bottom, and fortunately recovered it. At length, getting loose, they paddled ashore, and as it was already nearly dark, they encamped for the night. Mr Avery had all the matches upon his person when he swam ashore, consequently they were wet, and no fire could be obtained. This was the more disagreeable, as their clothes and blankets were all soaked with water. Although the weather was mild, they seldom suffered more; for the cold wet blankets chilled them through and through. Weary and exhausted, they could get no sleep. Wilson and Golden lay growling at each other all night.

In the morning they woke thoroughly chilled and more from the effects of sleeping on the hard clay bank and in wet

clothes. They had determined to abandon the raft, as the snags
and shoals were too frequent; and spreading their blankets in
the sun, remained in camp till they were dried. They employed
the time, however, in cutting down a large tree with hard nuts,
the kernels of which being extracted supplied them with four
days' provisions, that is, the means of sustaining life, for their
hardness and tastelessness hardly entitled them to the name of
food. While thus occupied, they discovered a saw-fish, about
two feet long, working his way up the shallow water, apparently
to enjoy the warmth of the sun. Strain shot him with a revolver,
and then jumping upon him succeeded in capturing him. Divided
between the four, he was but a scanty breakfast, but the meat
was sweet and palatable. They started at half past twelve from
'Saw-fish Camp', but after making two or three miles were
obliged to encamp, as both Mr Avery and Strain suffered extremely from sore legs. Exposed as they had been to the sun on
the raft for two days, Strain's, which were utterly unprotected,
were burnt to a blister in many places, while the undergrowth
and vines scratched and irritated them to such a degree, that it
produced a fever, which was followed by a chill. This looked
discouraging enough, especially as they saw no more indications
of approaching the Pacific than two weeks before. The bright
hopes with which the men had set out began to fade, and they
lay stretched about the bank, saying but little, but looking
moody and desponding. Strain spent the long afternoon pacing
slowly up and down the pebbly beach, pondering over the condition of his men, and vainly endeavouring to come to some conclusion respecting the future. However, with steel and powder,
they succeeded in obtaining a fire, which, sending its bright light
through the forest, imparted a little more cheerfulness to the
scene.

At half past seven next morning they set out, and moved
slowly down the left bank. Hearing a heavy report, they thought
it was a gun from the main body, and were much surprised at
the rapid progress it had made. About ten, after marching some
three miles, they halted on a shingle beach, where Mr Avery
was taken extremely ill with severe vomiting and retching.
While halting another gun was heard, supposed to be from the

main party, which Strain answered, hoping that they might come up, as he intended to leave Mr Avery with them and push on. At sunset, Mr Avery showing no signs of recovery, they went into camp No. 6. Fish were abundant in the stream, but they had no hook to catch them with, and so made their supper on hard nuts.

The next day they started early, but Avery's knee pained him severely. At times, exhausted with pain, he would cry out, 'Oh, Captain, hold on! hold on!' Strain would then stop and wait for him to limp up, but never went back. The necessities of the case were too stern to admit of a backward movement. Thus painfully marching – around swamps, through thickets, still on, towards an ocean that seemed infinitely removed – the half-naked, half-starved group cut their toilsome, disheartening way. At half past four they encamped on a shingle beach, having made about eight miles.

The following morning they started early, but were compelled to halt frequently for Avery, who would be left far behind, his extreme suffering causing faintness and sickness. Strain killed a fine wild turkey during the day, which gave them a good supper, though, when divided among four hungry men, the portion that each received appeared small. They also found an abundance of acid palm-nuts.

Next day the marching was more open and easy and they were fortunate enough to find clams. About 5.15 p.m. they encamped on a wet sand-beach. In cutting down some guinea-grass to protect them from dampness, Strain narrowly escaped being bitten by a large snake of the adder species; his machete cleaving the reptile just as he was about to strike. Every night a stick was set on the shore to see if there were any signs of tide. The eagerness with which this was inspected every morning showed the longing of the men for this indication of the proximity of the ocean. In the morning they thought they discovered a slight fall in the water, but found afterwards that they were mistaken.

The following day (February 22) the marching a part of the time was tolerably easy, but Wilson and Golden began to show signs of debility. Strain, nearly naked, went ahead and cleared a way with his cutlass. On finding the bushes too thick, he would plunge into them head foremost to break them down, trampling them under foot for those behind. During the day he killed another adder coiled to strike, but did not tell his men of it, lest they should become alarmed. Golden carrying no fire-arms, was often ordered forward to cut a path, but today he gave out completely, and when given the cutlass and directed to go to work, he laid the instrument down on the ground, then stretched himself beside it, and wept like a child. Destitution and toil were telling on him. He was a fine, splendid-looking young man, only twenty-two years of age, and brave as a lion; but this was a form of evil he had never dreamed of.

The next morning they proceeded on their journey through the woods and along the banks until one p.m., making about five miles, when they halted, as Strain had a most painful boil on his right instep, which prevented him from marching or wearing any boot. He was, moreover, suffering from a fall into a deep ravine the day before. About four o'clock, as they stretched around on the bank of the river, they were startled by a heavy booming sound, like that of a gun, which they thought at once came from Darien Harbour, the 'El Dorado' of the expedition. The delusion for a moment made every heart bound.

On 24 February Strain made a moccasin from a leather legging which formerly belonged to Truxton, who had proposed to boil it down and eat it. The former, however, prevented him saying they might yet need it for moccasins. So it turned out, and but for this very insignificant circumstance, it is very doubtful whether Strain could ever have got through at all, and consequently the whole party would have perished. On such simple suggestions, growing out of knowledge of a backwoods life, the fate of scores of men often depends. Slinging his spare boot to his blanket for future service, Strain gave the order to march at half past six, fondly hoping to reach Darien Harbour before night, but having travelled with great pain some eight miles, and seeing no signs of tide-water, at five o'clock encamped on a sand-bank. Having passed during the day two or three rapids with some ten or twelve feet fall, they consoled themselves with the reflection that this accounted for the absence of tides. During the day Strain killed a bird about the size of a partridge, which they ate raw.

The next morning they started early, but the long absence of food had so debilitated them that the marching was slow and difficult. They could make but short distances without being compelled to halt for a long rest. This tattered, skeleton group of four, stretched silent and sad in the forest beside that mysterious, unknown river, presented a most piteous spectacle. It is very doubtful whether the men ever would have started again but for the orders of their commander. As they staggered up to a jungle, Strain, after exhausting himself in clearing a path, would order the men to take their turn; but so feeble and dispirited were they, that often nothing but threats of the severest flogging could arouse them to make another effort for their lives. At length their attention was arrested by the cry of a wild animal. It proved to be the howling of a monkey, and the men, elated at the prospect of food, cried out, 'There's a monkey, Captain, shoot him!' 'Cut away,' replied Strain, thinking that the noise would excite its curiosity to come nearer. He was right, for the creature kept leaping from tree to tree, until at length it sat crouched on a limb directly above Strain, who was lying upon his back on the ground.

His carbine being damaged, he took the rifle belonging to Avery, and shooting nearly perpendicularly, sent a ball through the monkey's neck. The rifle, however, being loaded with stronger powder than usual, recoiled, cutting Strain's eyebrow and seriously endangering the eye itself. The monkey after receiving the wound, made off. Strain, though bleeding freely, fired again. His distrust of the rifle however, distracted his aim, when he drew a pistol and shot the creature through the heart. She fell over dead, but her tail would not uncoil, and she hung suspended from the limb. Strain then turned to take care of his eye, saying to the men, 'If you want that monkey you must cut down the tree.' Though tired and feeble, they attacked it with a will, and notwithstanding the trunk was three feet in circumference, and they had only a cutlass to work with, soon had it down.

This feast was on Sunday night, and the next morning at ten o'clock they pushed on; but the thick undergrowth was almost impassable, and after cutting for seven hours, making only three quarters of a mile per hour, they encamped on a damp clay bank. After two more days of marching they were too tired even to kindle a fire, but lay down in the darkness and slept on the cheerless bank of the stream. Strain now began to think of another raft, as all were so thoroughly debilitated, and so covered with boils, sores and scratches that they could not much longer cut their way through the jungle.

That night being unmolested by mosquitoes they had a quiet rest, and, though without food, began early in the morning to collect sticks for the raft; but the general debility, and want of proper tools and lashings, made their progress very slow, and it was sunset before they had enough brought together and lashed to float two persons. In the evening Mr Avery and Strain obtained some hard nuts and a small quantity of palmetto, which was all the food they had eaten for two days.

The next day Strain and Avery got on the raft, and the two floated slowly down the stream, while Golden and Wilson forced their way along the shore. Thus, two on the raft and two on the shore, they proceeded day after day – an occasional hallo, to ascertain each other's whereabouts, alone relieving the monotony of the hours. In making the bends sharp paddling was necessary, which, in their debilitated condition, was very exhausting. The second day they found a dead iguana, with the head eaten off. This they cooked and divided among them. The two men roasted the skin and chewed that. This miserable raft consisted of six half-decayed, broken trunks of trees lashed together with monkey skins and vines. Strain, half-naked and with his legs dangling in the water, sat on the forward end to steer, while his companion occupied the hinder part to assist. Now a tree in the distance chock-full of white cranes, and again a panther gazing on them with a bewildered stare, or young tigers, were the only objects that relieved the noiseless and apparently endless solitude. To pass away the time, Strain one day made Avery tell his history; at another time he would narrate from Don Quixote some amusing story. At length starvation produced the same singular effect on them that it did on Truxton and Maury, and they would spend hours in describing all the good dinners they had ever eaten. For the last two or three days, when most reduced, Strain said that he occupied almost all the whole time in arranging a magnificent dinner. Every luxury or curious dish that he had ever seen or heard of composed it, and he wore away the hours in going around his imaginary table, arranging and changing the several dishes.

On the 4th of March, however, as they sat on shore eating a portion of a dead tainted lizard, Strain heard a sudden roaring behind, and on looking up stream saw a rapid which they had just passed in smooth water. He knew at once that they must have floated over it at high tide, which now ebbing revealed the rift. It was clear they had at last reached tide-water. This was Strain's birthday, and he was looking out for some good luck. He, however, did not mention his discovery to the men, lest there should be some mistake. But they soon discovered it themselves, and cried out in transport, 'Oh, Captain, here is tide! here is tide!' That night Strain could not sleep until the time for flood-tide again arrived, and at eleven o'clock he took a firebrand and went down to the shore to see how it was going. The doubt was over – they had reached the swellings of the Pacific, and hope was rekindled in every bosom.

The time after this passed wearily. When it was flood-tide they lashed to the shore, and as the ebb commenced cut loose and slowly drifted down stream. At every turn they strained eagerly forward, hoping to get some look-out, or see some signs of civilization; but the same unbroken wilderness shut them in. Having ascertained how high the tide rose, Avery would take the Hudson River as a gauge, and prove conclusively that there was no great occasion for hope, as they were yet probably at least a hundred and fifty miles from the sea.

Anxious to get forward, they could not spend time to hunt; and a half dozen kernels of the palm nut, hard as ivory, would often constitute a meal. At length, on the 9th, Strain saw that food must be obtained, or the men would sink and die without making further progress. He therefore put Golden in his place with Avery on the raft, and taking Wilson with him struck into the woods to forage. Only four cartridges were left to them; and as Strain turned away with the rifle, Avery exclaimed, 'For God's sake, Strain, don't shoot at anything less than a turkey – remember that there are only four cartridges left!' After beating about for some time and finding nothing he came upon a partridge sitting on a limb. The temptation was too strong to be resisted, and he drew up and killed it. His conscience smote him the moment he had done so, as on that single cartridge might yet hang the lives of all the party. At length, however, he came upon a grove of palm nuts. By tightening his cartridge-belt around him, and filling his flannel shirt above it with nuts, he soon had all he could carry, and turned back to the river. But the two got entangled in a swamp, and were wholly exhausted before they could extricate themselves. Wilson then began to beg for the partridge; but Strain told him it was for the party, and must be divided equally. The man at length fell down, and said he could and would go no farther without that partridge. Strain threw it to him, saying 'Take it,' and sat down on a log to see him devour it. At length they reached the river, and kept down the bank. About three o'clock, Strain was startled by Wilson's exclaiming, 'My God, sir, there is the raft!' and sure enough, there it was, deserted and floating quietly in the middle of the river awaiting the action of the tide (it was then slack water) to determine its course.

The sight of that abandoned structure at first struck like an ice-bolt to the heart of both, but a single glance showed Strain that the blankets, spare arms, etc., had been taken away, and another, that about eight feet of rope, which had been used to lash the logs, was left untouched, while one of the paddles still remained. He concluded at once that the party had either obtained assistance and left the raft – in which case they would not require, and would probably neglect, the lashings – or that they had been murdered by Indians, who had left the raft adrift for the purpose of entrapping the remainder. In answer to Wilson's anxious inquiries, he frankly told him his conjectures. 'Well, sir,' replied Wilson, 'if there be Indians about, you have three cartridges left, and are certain of three men, and I think with my machete I can give an account of two more.' This was the ring of true metal and pleased Strain much. While awaiting the progress of the raft, which drifted slowly towards their side of the river, they passed their leisure time in eating nuts. Finally, seeing it foul of some drift-wood about one hundred yards below, they after some difficulty got upon it, and proceeded with the current down the river. Strain, however, first made a thorough examination, to see if there was any blood or other evidence of a struggle upon it, or a note from Mr Avery which might unravel the mystery.

After drifting half an hour they saw a clearing on the left bank; and soon after, in passing the mouth of a small stream on the same side, discovered two canoes approaching rapidly from below.

Not feeling assured that the paddlers were not Indians, who might prove hostile, as they were coloured and spoke loudly in a dialect which, at a distance, he could not understand, Strain determined to keep them at arms' length until assured of their peaceable intentions. He accordingly hailed when they came within rifleshot, and asked who they were and where they were going. They replied, in Spanish, that they were friends, had just taken off his companions, and brought a letter to himself. True to his naval principles, never to let an enemy approach too near without declaring his intentions, Strain sat across the log and hailed as though he trod the deck of a man-of-war. These two skeletons on a mass of drift-wood thus demanding explanations, were very much like a shipwrecked mariner lashed to a spar bidding a vessel stand off till she showed her colours. When convinced, however, of the peaceable intentions of the natives, they gladly abandoned the raft and entered the canoe. Finding that the boatmen had tobacco and a pipe, Strain immediately borrowed them, and, for the first time since the 4th of February, enjoyed the luxury of a smoke.

It was just dark when they reached the village of Yavisa. The excitement was over – the immediate necessity of effort past, and Strain's over-tasked nature gave way. He could no longer walk, and was helped by two men to the house of the Sub-Alcalde, where he met Mr Avery and Golden. When the commander of the United States Darien Exploring Expedition entered the Alcalde's house, his uniform consisted of a blue flannel shirt, one boot, and a Panama hat, none of which articles was in a very good condition.

Strain would not rest. He went on by canoe, and luckily he found an English warship. Within a week he set off up the river again, with some of the English sailors in a ship's boat, and a party of natives in canoes.

The tide and some fourteen English oarsmen propelled them rapidly up the stream, and they only halted when it became so dark that they could proceed no farther. While at anchor near the bank, an incident occurred which had nearly proved fatal to the expedition and all engaged, and for a moment seemed to indicate that destiny was against them, and that the unfortunate party had been marked for destruction. At eleven o'clock at night, when all were asleep in the boat except the two sentries and Strain, the latter heard amidst the profound stillness a cracking and rending of timber in the woods, which he knew at once to proceed from a falling tree. He first thought it was some distance from the bank, but on looking up to see whether it was likely to strike and bring down any other timber nearer the shore, he saw against the starlit sky, directly over his head, the dark and swaying form of a tree gradually declining towards the spot where the unsuspecting boats lay moored. His first thought was, 'My poor men will now be lost!' He, however, never opened his mouth, but watched the descending mass without moving, as it came directly towards him. Suddenly, as if turned aside by some unseen hand, it inclined to the right, and fell with a fearful crash into the river, a few feet behind, tearing off a piece of the stern of one of the canoes which was moored alongside. Shouts and exclamations followed, and for a moment the greatest consternation prevailed among the seamen, who thought the Indians were upon them but the voices of the officers, and assurances that the danger had passed, soon restored order. Mr Avery, who slept in a canoe alongside, had a narrow escape; but fortunately a good wetting was all the inconvenience which any of them experienced.

Next day was Sunday, and all were early at work and advancing up the river. About midday they were joined by two canoes containing eleven natives, who had been dispatched after them from Yavisa. At two o'clock they arrived as far as the boat could go, and after a hasty dinner, embarked the officers and a portion of the men in the canoes.

At dark they encamped on a shingle beach, and, after a hearty supper, set the watch, which consisted of one officer and two sentries. The remainder were soon asleep around the watchfires.

As rapids were becoming frequent, one of the native canoes was detailed to assist the English to stem the strong current, which they did by dragging them over by hand. The other was permitted to go ahead for the purpose of hunting in which the men were very expert. Passing several well-recognized camps of his downward progress, and intervals which it had cost him days of hard labour to accomplish, they encamped after sunset, the 21st of March, on the rocky beach upon which Strain had slept the 16th of February, after having abandoned his raft in the morning.

As they continued to ascend they saw small crosses along the banks, erected, according to previous arrangement, by the main party as they descended, to point out to Strain their progress when he should return with assistance. But the signs soon ceased, and although they passed numerous return camps, there was no symbol from which it could be inferred that they had the remotest hope of relief from below. Worn-out belts and cartridge boxes, found in camps on the river, showed that the party were dispensing with all unnecessary weight, while pieces of leather cut from the latter gave evidence that their boots and shoes were nearly worn out. Quills and feathers of the loathsome buzzard scattered along, revealed the character of food to which stern necessity had at last driven them. In the afternoon they arrived at the camp from whence Strain had taken leave of the party, and found that it had been revisited by them, the evidence of which was the remains of a fire and some cartridge boxes which had been discarded. About sunset they encamped on a sloping bank, and passed a night of torture, owing to the myriads of mosquitoes which infested the camp.

This was a sad night for Strain. From the examination of today's camp it was evident his command had given him up for lost, and commenced the desperate undertaking of finding their way back to the Atlantic shore.

At early daylight, when the sand-flies relieved the night-guard of mosquitoes, they rose to prepare for a day of labour and excitement, as Strain had every reason to believe he should overtake the main body of his party before night. As they were now nearly in the heart of the Isthmus, and might possibly meet Indians, a regular order of sailing was adopted, and the canoes followed each other in close order.

For some hours, early in the afternoon, they lost sight of the return camps, and the English party, officers as well as men, became apprehensive that the party had abandoned the river. But on this subject Strain felt no anxiety, as he knew that they would not dare to leave the stream, which was their only guide and the only certain source from which they could obtain water. Nearly the whole of this day they fired their muskets and shouted at short intervals, in order to attract their attention should they be pursuing their march in the forest, where it was generally more free from undergrowth than close to the river bank.

Signs of disorganization, however, now became more alarming, and the evidence of extreme debility and starvation more apparent. Buzzards' quills, haversacks, fragments of clothing strewed along, together with the want of order in the camps, and their close proximity, attested that the little band had well-nigh reached the end of their march. With every fresh symptom of extreme destitution Strain became more painfully agitated, for the dreadful fear that they had been compelled to resort to cannibalism haunted him, and made him tremble to proceed. But nerving himself to the worst, and keeping his forebodings to himself, he pushed on and soon after announced a camp less than three days old. This was responded to by a loud cheer and a discharge of firearms. Even the natives began to feel the excitement, and bent to their paddles with lustier strokes. They had not proceeded far before another camp was found, the ashes of which were declared to be warm; and then the excitement reached the highest pitch. Shout after shout went up, shot after shot rang through the forest, and a common enthusiasm and ardour inspired every breast.

At about sunset the natives, who were ahead in the scout canoe, announced a smoke in sight, and immediately after making a turn in the river Strain discovered five men standing on the shelving beach just out of the wood. He immediately discharged his musket to warn them of his approach, lest the effect of too sudden joy might be fatal; and then cheer after cheer echoed and re-echoed through the forest, as each canoe in succession swept round the point and caught sight of the motionless forms in the distance.

When Strain saw but five men his heart sank with dread, and he exclaimed, 'My God, is that all!' but the next moment a faint cheer from the forest in the rear announced that others still remained alive. His canoe swept with a bound to the shore; but before its prow grated upon it he was on the land. His first inquiry was, 'How many men have you lost?' 'Five,' was the answer.

Several of the poor men there had heard the shouts of deliverance, but the joyful intelligence could not impart strength to their wasted frames. There they lay – lacerated, ulcerated frames of men half-covered with rags. Each turned his eye as his commander approached, but none could get up.

The perfect composure and resignation which reigned in that ghastly group, gave tenfold impressiveness to the scene. But no description can convey any adequate impression of its true character. The British officers were shocked beyond measure, and the surgeon declared that though he had seen much of suffering, in hospitals and elsewhere, he never before dreamed that men could live and march in such a state of emaciation and destitution.

The party were three days in regaining the English ship's boat. As they approached it, Strain wished to hoist the American ensign, and asked if the one they started with had been preserved. They answered yes. One of the men had wrapped it round his breast, and though weapons, haversacks, and blankets had been thrown away, he would never part with it.

Unbinding it with his skeleton hand from the rags that but hardly covered him, he gave it, tattered and torn, to the wind, and three cheers went up from the little fleet.

– from *Harper's New Monthly Magazine*, March 1855

# DAVID HOWARTH

# Stuck in the Mud

'Hullo, Howarth,' the Training Lieutenant-Commander said, 'I'm delighted to see you. Now you can tell us all the mistakes we're making.' This was an unexpected greeting. It was the middle of World War II, and I was only a sub-lieutenant; and I was joining his ship (or so I thought) for a short beginner's course in one-man submarines. She was a converted merchant ship, lying in a sea-loch in the west of Scotland, and we were standing on deck among a litter of baby submarines. I had never seen one before, or been to sea in any kind of submarine.

The lieutenant-commander took me to the wardroom and gave me some gin and said: 'The trouble with you experts is that you don't come to see us often enough.'

I really did try hard to tell him I was not an expert, at least not in one-man submarines, but he only thought I was pretending to be modest.

'Anyone can drive them,' he said. 'What we want to know is what you backroom boys are going to use them for.'

There is a moral to this story, and I might as well state it right away: never let your head be turned by flattery, even from someone so superior as a lieutenant-commander. The trouble was that I did know what his submarines were going to be used for. In fact, I had been told to plan an attack by them, and that was why I had asked for a chance to try them for myself. But the plans were top secret, and I had not been told I could tell him about them. The more secretive I became the more he was convinced that I knew all there was to be known about midget submarines.

Looking back, I can see it was only common sense for him to think that anyone making operational plans for a specialized weapon would know how the weapon worked. But things that happen in wartime are not always guided by common sense.

Anyhow, I almost began to believe what he seemed to imply: that driving the things was just child's play for someone as clever as me. To be on the safe side, I did persuade him to lend me a diagram, and I studied it that night in my cabin.

The submarine was about fifteen feet long, so far as I remember, and about two feet in diameter, with a steel dome in the middle with narrow horizontal slit windows in it. You sat with your legs in the body of it and your head in the dome. The basic controls were certainly simple. There was an aircraft control column for steering horizontally and up and down, and a speed control for the electric motor. Above one's head in the dome there was a lever which let air out of the ballast tanks to submerge, and down on the right was a small knob which let compressed air out of a cylinder to blow the tanks when you wanted to surface.

There were a lot of other gadgets connected with the submarine's operational use – for example, controls to release its explosive warhead; but I didn't think I would havt to bother with them on a practice trip. There was also a sea-cock which would flood the submarine in an emergency, until the pressure inside was equal to the pressure outside. Then, in theory, you could open the lid of the dome and escape.

The lieutenant-commander pointed it out to me.

'I shouldn't turn that unless you really want to,' he said. 'Nobody's tried it yet.'

So the next morning, when I was handed over to a chief petty officer and a submarine was hoisted over the side for me, I went down the ladder sodden with flattery and confidence.

'What's your weight, sir?' the C.P.O. asked me.

'About one hundred and fifty pounds,' I said. I didn't pause to wonder why he had asked me. I climbed into the open dome and wriggled down inside. For someone over six feet, it was like getting into a small sports car.

The C.P.O. took my cap. Obviously, there wouldn't be room for it on my head when the lid was shut.

'Better submerge alongside for a couple of feet, sir,' he said. 'Just to check her trim.'

Then he clanged the lid down on top of me and I locked it. It completely shut off the sounds from outside, the bustle and voices and machinery and the lap of water.

There was a narrow view through the slit windows, a few inches above the water. I recognized the control column between my knees, and the knobs and the levers from the drawing. There was a depth gauge, and a compass. I felt above my head and pulled the lever to submerge, and the boat slowly began to sink. Small waves lapped against the windows, then the water covered them, and I saw the curious sight of the surface of the sea from underneath.

I had only looked at it for a second or two when I realized it was disappearing out of sight above me. Then there was nothing outside but a milky green light. That seemed to be fading rather quickly. Slightly surprised, I looked at the depth gauge. It said twenty-five feet, and the needle was going round as fast as the second hand of a watch. Before I had collected my wits, everything was absolutely pitch black, except for the needle of the depth gauge, which was luminous. I watched it go right round the dial to fifty feet, which was as far as it could go.

The boat went on sinking. I started the motor and pulled the control column right back. But nothing seemed to happen. At last, there was a very faint jar, and the boat tilted down by the nose. She was on the bottom.

I think it was the abruptness of it all that was most alarming, the sudden transition from the cheerful activity and the sunlight and the paternal C.P.O. and my own ridiculous self-confidence: from that to the absolute darkness and silence of the bottom of the sea, to being irretrievably locked in and alone in a space so confined that one couldn't move more than a man in a coffin.

I didn't know what had gone wrong, and in that total darkness I had no hope of finding out. But anyhow I remembered the diagram. There were three knobs on the right hand side, and the middle one was the one which blew the tanks. I felt for them and found the middle one and tried to turn it. It would not turn at all. I tried to think of all the air cocks I had seen. I pushed it and pulled it, and tried to turn it backwards, but it would not move in any direction, and nothing happened. The panic of being shut in is a most unpleasant sensation. It started to rise in me, and I started to talk to myself, which I do not remember ever having done before or since. I am not sure if I spoke out loud, but I said: 'If you keep your head there must be a way out of this. If you don't, there isn't.' I *knew* that was the right knob. It *must* turn anti-clockwise. There was no reason why they should have fitted any other kind of knob.

I felt it all over very carefully. It was very small, about the size of a radio knob, and there were two thin pipes leading away from it, but I could not reach far enough to trace where they went to. It seemed a fragile thing, and if it was the right cock it was full of high pressure air. I could feel it all bend when I twisted it hard, and I was afraid if I tried too hard I would break it and be killed stone dead by the air pressure it would release in the hull of the boat.

But after another long pause to think, I couldn't see any alternative to brute force. I took off my shoe and hit the knob. That did no good. Then I took out my handkerchief and twisted it round the knob to get a better grip and put all my strength on it.

Suddenly something gave way. And after taking a second to discover I wasn't dead, I heard air hissing into the tanks.

After it had hissed for a bit, it began to bubble, and I guessed that the tanks were full of air and overflowing. I turned the air off, and the dead silence returned. But the nose stayed tilted down. I waited, in the hope that she was rising slowly, but I really knew what had happened: even with full buoyancy, she was still stuck in the mud.

I tried to rock her from side to side, but in the dark I could not tell if she was moving. The effort made me breathe faster, and I thought of the oxygen I was using, so I stopped and just sat there. I could not think of anything to do.

I wondered about the sea-cock which no-one had ever tried. But even if I had had the courage to open it and sit there while she flooded, I was sure I was much too deep to get up to the surface without an escape apparatus. And in that at least I was right: I looked up the depth on the chart afterwards, and it was 78 feet.

I also wondered how long the air would last, and how long it would take the crew up above to find me and haul me up again, if they could find me at all. But that did not need much thought. It was obvious the air would be finished first.

It was the only time in my life, so far, that I expected to die within a few minutes and couldn't think of anything to do about it. But I did not think any serious thoughts about dying. I was puzzling over the technical problems. The clue to what had happened, I now understood, had been in the C.P.O.'s question about my weight. There must have been some adjustment he could have made to compensate for the different weights of different people. It was years since I had weighed myself, and when I answered him so casually I had told him a weight that was far too low. But the damage was done, and there was nothing I could do to correct it.

Suddenly, for no reason at all, I felt her come unstuck.

She went up nearly as quickly as she had gone down. When she got to 50 feet, the depth gauge gave a jerk, and began to fall so fast that a new worry put all the others out of my head. I remembered the ship above me. What would happen if I hit it hard on its bottom? I imagined getting tangled up under its keel, with the submarine dented and leaking. So I let out some air from the tanks, and the rate of ascent slowed down.

Just as it was getting light, the depth gauge stopped moving and I glanced out of the slit and saw an enormous propeller a few feet in front of me, and then she began to sink again. This time she went slower, but she was on the bottom again before I could get the air knob to turn.

I escaped in the end: otherwise I would not be writing this shameful story. The next time I got the submarine to rise, I was beginning to get the hang of her. She came up at a more reasonable speed, and I steadied her at 30 feet and started the motor. I put her on a compass course towards the middle of the loch and waited a couple of minutes. Then I blew the tanks and bobbed up like a cork. I had been down there about half an hour, which was much too long for anybody's comfort.

I looked out of the little window, and saw the ship. Scores of men of her crew were lining the rail, staring down at the spot where I had sunk. Then one or two of them saw me and pointed, and all of them lost interest and wandered away. I motored towards her, and saw the Lieutenant-Commander looking rather pale and not very pleased. The Chief Petty Officer lifted the lid off me.

'Thought you was drowned, sir,' he said.

He was still holding my cap.

# WINSTON CHURCHILL

# I Escape from the Boers

In 1899, during the Boer War, Winston Churchill was War
Correspondent for a London newspaper. He was twenty-five, and
had already seen battle as an officer in India and the Sudan.
During a skirmish he was captured by the Boers and imprisoned
in their capital, Pretoria, in a school which had been converted
into a prison camp.

The State Model Schools stood in the midst of a quadrangle, and
were surrounded on two sides by an iron grille and on two
by a corrugated-iron fence about ten feet high. These boundaries offered little obstacle to anyone who possessed the activity
of youth, but the fact that they were guarded on the inside by
sentries, fifty yards apart, armed with rifle and revolver, made
them a well-nigh insuperable barrier. No walls are so hard to
pierce as living walls.

'After anxious reflection and continual watching, it was discovered by several of the prisoners that when the sentries along
the eastern side walked about on their beats they were at certain
moments unable to see the top of a few yards of the wall near
the small circular lavatory office ... the electric lights in the
middle of the quadrangle brilliantly lighted the whole place, but
the eastern wall was in shadow. The first thing was therefore to
pass the two sentries near the office. It was necessary to hit off
the exact moment when both their backs should be turned together. After the wall was scaled we should be in the garden of
the villa next door. There the plan came to an end. Everything
after this was vague and uncertain. How to get out of the garden, how to pass unnoticed through the streets, how to evade
the patrols that surrounded the town, and above all how to
cover the two hundred and eighty miles to the Portuguese
frontier, were questions which would arise at a later stage.

'Together with Captain Haldane and Lieutenant Brockie I made
an abortive attempt, not pushed with any decision, on 11 Decem-

ber. There was no difficulty in getting into the circular office. But to climb out of it over the wall was a hazard of the sharpest character. Anyone doing so must at the moment he was on the top of the wall be plainly visible to the sentries fifteen yards away, if they were in the right place and happened to look! Whether the sentries would challenge or fire depended entirely upon their individual dispositions, and no one could tell what they would do. Nevertheless I was determined that nothing should stop my taking the plunge the next day. As the 12th wore away my fears crystallized more and more into desperation. In the evening, after my two friends had made an attempt, but had not found the moment propitious, I strolled across the quadrangle and secreted myself in the circular office. Through an aperture in the metal casing of which it was built I watched the sentries. For some time they remained stolid and obstructive. Then all of a sudden one turned and walked up to his comrade, and they began to talk. Their backs were turned.

'Now or never! I stood on a ledge, seized the top of the wall with my hands, and drew myself up. Twice I let myself down in sickly hesitation, and then with a third resolve scrambled up and over. My waistcoat got entangled with the ornamental metal-work on the top. I had to pause for an appreciable moment to extricate myself. In this posture I had one parting glimpse of the sentries still talking with their backs turned fifteen yards away. One of them was lighting his cigarette, and I remember the glow on the inside of his hands as a distinct impression which my mind recorded. Then I lowered myself lightly down into the adjoining garden and crouched among the shrubs. I was free! The first step had been taken, and it was irrevocable. It now remained to await the arrival of my comrades. The bushes in the garden gave a deal of cover, and in the moonlight their shadows fell dark on the ground. I lay here for an hour in great impatience and anxiety. People were continually moving about in the garden, and once a man came and apparently looked straight at me only a few yards away. Where were the others? Why did they not make the attempt?

'Suddenly I heard a voice from within the quadrangle say,

quite loud, "All up." I crawled back to the wall. Two officers were walking up and down inside, jabbering Latin words, laughing and talking all manner of nonsense – amid which I caught my name. I risked a cough. One of the officers immediately began to chatter alone. The other said, slowly and clearly, "They cannot get out. The sentry suspects. It's all up. Can you get back again?" But now all my fears fell from me at once. To go back was impossible. I could not hope to climb the wall unnoticed. There was no helpful ledge on the outside. Fate pointed onwards. Besides, I said to myself, "Of course, I shall be recaptured, but I will at least have a run for my money", I said to the officers, "I shall go on alone".

'Now I was in the right mood for these undertakings – failure being almost certain, no odds against success affected me. All risks were less than the certainty ... The gate which led into the road was only a few yards from another sentry. I said to myself, "Toujours de l'audace", put my hat on my head, strode into the middle of the garden, walked past the windows of the house without any attempt at concealment, and so went through the gate and turned to the left. I passed the sentry at less than five yards. Most of them knew me by sight. Whether he looked at me or not I do not know, for I never turned my head. I restrained with the utmost difficulty an impulse to run. But after walking a hundred yards and hearing no challenge, I knew that the second obstacle had been surmounted. I was at large in Pretoria.

'I walked on leisurely through the night, humming a tune and choosing the middle of the road. The streets were full of burghers, but they paid no attention to me. Gradually I reached the suburbs, and on a little bridge I sat down to reflect and consider. I was in the heart of the enemy's country. I knew no one to whom I could apply for succour. Nearly three hundred miles stretched between me and Delagoa Bay. My escape must be known at dawn. Pursuit would be immediate. Yet all exits were barred. The town was picketed, the country was patrolled, the trains were searched, the line was guarded. I wore a civilian brown flannel suit. I had seventy-five pounds in my pocket and four slabs of chocolate, but the compass and the map which might have guided me, the opium tablets and meat lozenges which should have sustained me, were in my friends' pockets in the State Model Schools. Worst of all, I could not speak a word of Dutch or Kaffir, and how was I to get food or direction?

'But when hope had departed, fear had gone as well. I formed a plan. I would find the Delagoa Bay Railway. Without map or compass, I must follow that in spite of the pickets. I looked at the stars. Orion shone brightly. Scarcely a year before he had guided me when lost in the desert to the banks of the Nile. He had given me water. Now he should lead to freedom. I could not endure the want of either.

'After walking south for half a mile I struck the railway. Was it the line to Delagoa Bay or the Pietersburg branch? If it were the former, it should run east. But, so far as I could see, this line ran northwards. Still, it might be only winding its way out among the hills. I resolved to follow it. The night was delicious. A cool breeze fanned my face, and a wild feeling of exhilaration took hold of me. At any rate, I was free, if only for an hour. That was something. The fascination of the adventure grew. Unless the stars in their courses fought for me, I could not escape. Where, then, was the need of caution? I marched briskly along the line. Here and there the lights of a picket fire gleamed. Every bridge had its watchers. But I passed them all, making very short detours at the dangerous places, and really taking scarcely any precautions. Perhaps that was the reason I succeeded.

'As I walked I extended my plan. I could not march three hundred miles to the frontier. I would board a train in motion and hide under the seats, on the roof, on the couplings – anywhere. I thought of Paul Bultitude's escape from school in *Vice Versa*. I saw myself emerging from under the seat, and bribing or persuading some fat first-class passenger to help me. What train should I take? The first, of course. After walking for two hours I perceived the signal lights of a station. I left the line, and circling round it, hid in the ditch by the track about two hundred yards beyond the platform. I argued that the train would stop at the station and that it would not have got up too much speed by the time it reached me. An hour passed. I began to grow impatient. Suddenly I heard the whistle and the approaching rattle. Then the great yellow headlights of the engine flashed into view. The train waited five minutes at the station, and started again with much noise and steaming. I crouched by the track. I rehearsed the act in my mind. I must wait until the engine had passed, otherwise I should be seen. Then I must make a dash for the carriages.

'The train started slowly, but gathered speed sooner than I had expected. The flaring lights drew swiftly near. The rattle became a roar. The dark mass hung for a second above me. The engine-driver silhouetted against his furnace glow, the black profile of the engine, the clouds of steam rushed past. Then I hurled myself on the trucks, clutched at something, missed, clutched again, missed again, grasped some sort of hand-hold, was swung off my feet – my toes bumping on the line, and with a struggle seated myself on the couplings of the fifth truck from the front of the train. It was a goods train, and the trucks were full of sacks, soft sacks covered with coal-dust. They were in fact bags filled with empty coal bags going back to their colliery. I crawled on top and burrowed in among them. In five minutes I was completely buried. The sacks were warm and comfortable. Perhaps the engine-driver had seen me rush up to the train and would give the alarm at the next station; on the other hand, perhaps not. Where was the train going to? Where would it be unloaded? Would it be searched? Was it on the Delagoa Bay line? What should I do in the morning? Ah, never mind that. Sufficient for the night was the luck thereof. Fresh plans for fresh contingencies. I resolved to sleep, nor can I imagine a more pleasing lullaby than the clatter of the train that carries an escaping prisoner at twenty miles an hour away from the enemy's capital.

'How long I slept I do not know, but I woke up suddenly with all feelings of exhilaration gone, and only the conscious-ness of oppressive difficulties heavy on me. I must leave the train before daybreak, so that I could drink at a pool and find some hiding-place while it was still dark. I would not run the risk of being unloaded with the coal bags. Another night I would board another train. I crawled from my cosy hiding-place among the sacks and sat again on the couplings. The train was running at a fair speed, but I felt it was time to leave it. I took hold of the iron handle at the back of the truck, pulled strongly with my left hand, and sprang. My feet struck the ground in two gigantic strides, and the next instant I was sprawling in the ditch considerably shaken but unhurt. The train, my faithful ally of the night, hurried on its journey.

'It was still dark. I was in the middle of a wide valley, surrounded by low hills, and carpeted with high grass drenched in dew. I searched for water in the nearest gully, and soon found a clear pool. I was very thirsty, but long after I had quenched my thirst I continued to drink, that I might have sufficient for the whole day.

'Presently the dawn began to break, and the sky to the east grew yellow and red, slashed across with heavy black clouds. I saw with relief that the railway ran steadily towards the sunrise. I had taken the right line, after all.

'Having drunk my fill, I set out for the hills, among which I hoped to find some hiding-place, and as it became broad daylight I entered a small grove of trees which grew on the side of a deep ravine. Here I resolved to wait till dusk. I had one consolation: no one in the world knew where I was – I did not know myself. It was now four o'clock. Fourteen hours lay between me and the night. My impatience to proceed while I was still strong doubled their length. At first it was terribly cold, but by degrees the sun gained power, and by ten o'clock the heat was oppressive. My sole companion was a gigantic vulture, who manifested an extravagant interest in my condition, and made hideous and ominous gurglings from time to time. From my lofty position I commanded a view of the whole valley. A little tin-roofed town lay three miles to the westward. Scattered farmsteads, each with a clump of trees, relieved the monotony of the undulating ground. At the foot of the hill stood a Kaffir kraal, and the figures of its inhabitants dotted the patches of cultivation or surrounded the droves of goats and cows which fed on the pasture ... During the day I ate one slab of chocolate, which, with the heat, produced a violent thirst. The pool was hardly half a mile away, but I dared not leave the shelter of the little wood, for I could see figures of white men riding or walking occasionally across the valley, and once a Boer came and fired two shots at birds close to my hiding-place. But no one discovered me.

'The elation and the excitement of the previous night had burnt away, and a chilling reaction followed. I was very hungry, for I had no dinner before starting, and chocolate, though it sustains, does not satisfy. I had scarcely slept, but yet my heart beat so fiercely and I was so nervous and perplexed about the future that I could not rest. I thought of all the chances that lay against me: I dreaded and detested more than words can express the prospect of being caught and dragged back to Pretoria. I found no comfort in any of the philosophical ideas which some men parade in their hours of ease and strength and safety. They seemed only fair-weather friends. I realized with awful force that no exercise of my own feeble wit and strength could save me from my enemies, and that without the assistance of that High Power which interferes in the eternal sequence of causes and effects more often than we are prone to admit, I could never succeed. I prayed long and earnestly for help and guidance. My prayer, as it seems to me, was swiftly and wonderfully answered.'

I wrote these lines many years ago while the impression of the adventure was strong upon me. Then I could tell no more. To have done so would have compromised the liberty and perhaps the lives of those who had helped me. For many years these reasons have disappeared. The time has come when I can relate the events which followed, and which changed my nearly hopeless position into one of superior advantage.

During the day I had watched the railway with attention. I saw two or three trains pass along it each way, I argued that the same number would pass at night: I resolved to board one of these. I thought I could improve on my procedure of the previous evening. I had observed how slowly the trains, particularly long goods-trains, climbed some of the steep gradients. Sometimes they were hardly going at a foot's pace. It would probably be easy to choose a point where the line was not only on an up-grade but also on a curve. Thus I could board some truck on the convex side of the train when both the engine and the guard's van were bent away, and when consequently neither the engine-driver nor the guard would see me. This plan seemed to me in every respect sound. I saw myself leaving the train again before dawn, having been carried forward another sixty or seventy miles during the night. That would be scarcely one hundred and fifty miles from the frontier. And why should not the process be repeated? Where was the flaw? I could not see it. With three long bounds on three successive nights I could be in Portuguese territory. Meanwhile I still had two or three slabs of chocolate and a pocketful of crumbled biscuit – enough, that is to say, to keep body and soul together at a pinch without running the awful risk of recapture entailed by accosting a single human being. In this mood I watched with increasing impatience the arrival of darkness.

The long day reached its close at last. The western clouds flushed into fire; the shadows of the hills stretched out across the valley; a ponderous Boer wagon with its long team crawled slowly along the track towards the township, the Kaffirs collected their herds and drew them round their Kraal; the daylight died, and soon it was quite dark. Then, and not until then, I set forth. I hurried to the railway line, scrambling along through the boulders and high grass and pausing on my way to drink at a stream of sweet cold water. I made my way to the place where I had seen the trains crawling so slowly up the slope and soon found a point where the curve of the track fulfilled all the conditions of my plan. Here, behind a little bush, I sat down and waited hopefully. An hour passed; two hours passed; three hours – and yet no train. Six hours had now elapsed since the last, whose time I had carefully noted, had gone by. Surely one was due. Another hour slipped away. Still no train! My plan began to crumble and my hopes to ooze out of me. After all, was it not quite possible that no trains ran on this part of the line during the dark hours? This was in fact the case, and I might well have continued to wait in vain till daylight. However, between twelve and one in the morning I lost patience and started along the track, resolved to cover at any rate ten or fifteen miles of my journey. I did not make much progress. Every bridge was guarded by armed men; every few miles were huts. At intervals there were stations with tin-roofed villages clustering around them. All the veldt was bathed in the bright rays of the full moon, and to avoid these dangerous places I had to make wide circuits and even to creep along the ground. Leaving the railroad I fell into bogs and swamps, brushed through high grass dripping with dew, and waded across the streams over which the bridges carried the railway. I was soon drenched to the waist. I had been able to take very little exercise during my month's imprisonment, and I was quickly tired with walking and with want of food and sleep. Presently I approached a station. It was a mere platform in the veldt, with two or three buildings and huts around it. But laid up on the sidings, obviously for the night, were three long goods-trains. Evidently the flow of traffic over the railway was uneven. These three trains, motionless in the moonlight, confirmed my fears that traffic was not maintained by night on this part of the line. Where then, was my plan which in the afternoon had looked so fine and sure?

It now occurred to me that I might board one of these stationary trains immediately, and hiding amid its freight be carried forward during the next day – and night too if all were well. On the other hand, where were they going to? Where would they stop? Where would they be unloaded? Once I entered a wagon my lot would be cast. I might find myself ignominiously unloaded and recaptured at Witbank or Middleburg, or at any station in the long two hundred miles which separated me from the frontier. It was necessary at all costs before taking such a step to find out where these trains were going. To do this I must penetrate the station, examine the labels on the trucks or on the merchandise, and see if I could extract any certain guidance from them. I crept up to the platform and got between two of the long trains on the siding. I was proceeding to examine the markings on the trucks when loud voices rapidly approaching on the outside of the trains filled me with fear. Several Kaffirs were laughing and shouting in their unmodulated tones, and I heard, as I thought, a European voice arguing or ordering. At any rate, it was enough for me. I retreated between the two trains to the extreme end of the siding, and slipped stealthily but rapidly into the grass of the illimitable plain.

There was nothing for it but to plod on – but in an increasingly purposeless and hopeless manner. I felt very miserable when I looked around and saw here and there the lights and houses and thought of the warmth and comfort within them, but knew that they meant only danger to me. Far off, on the moonlit horizon there presently began to shine the row of six or eight big lights which marked either Witbank or Middleburg station. Out in the darkness to my left gleamed two or three fires. I was sure they were not the lights of houses, but how far off they were or what they were I could not be certain. The idea formed in my mind that they were the fires of a Kaffir kraal. Then I began to think that the best use I could make of my remaining strength would be to go to these Kaffirs. I had heard that they hated the Boers and were friendly to the British. At any rate, they would probably not arrest me. They might give me food and a dry corner to sleep in. Although I could not speak a word of their language, yet I thought perhaps they might understand the value of a British banknote. They might even be induced to help me. A guide, a pony – but, above all, rest, warmth, and food – such were the promptings which dominated my mind. So I set out towards the fires.

I must have walked a mile or so in this resolve before a realization of its weakness and impudence took possession of me. Then I turned back again to the railway line and retraced my steps perhaps half the distance. Then I stopped and sat down, completely baffled, destitute of any idea what to do or where to turn. Suddenly without the slightest reason all my doubts disappeared. It was certainly by no process of logic that they were dispelled. I just felt quite clear that I would go to the Kaffir kraal. I had sometimes in former years held a 'Planchette' pencil and written while others had touched my wrist or hand. I acted in exactly the same unconscious or subconscious manner now.

I walked on rapidly towards the fires, which I had in the first instance thought were not more than a couple of miles from the railway line. I soon found they were much farther away than that. After about an hour or an hour and a half they still seemed almost as far off as ever. But I persevered, and presently between two and three o'clock in the morning I perceived that they were not the fires of a Kaffir kraal. The angular outline of buildings began to draw out against them, and soon I saw that I was approaching a group of houses around the mouth of a coal-mine. The wheel which worked the winding gear was plainly visible, and I could see that the fires which had led me so far were from the furnaces of the engines. Hard by, surrounded by one or two slighter structures, stood a small but substantial stone house two storeys high.

I halted in the wilderness to survey this scene and to revolve my action. It was still possible to turn back. But in that direction I saw nothing but the prospect of further futile wanderings terminated by hunger, fever, discovery, or surrender. On the other hand, here in front was a chance. I had heard it said before I escaped that in the mining district of Witbank and Middleburg there was a certain number of English residents who had been suffered to remain in the country in order to keep the mines working. Had I been led to one of these? What did this house which frowned dark and inscrutable upon me contain? A Briton or a Boer; a friend or a foe? Nor did this exhaust the possibilities. I had my seventy-five pounds in English notes in my pocket. If I revealed my identity I thought that I could give reasonable assurance of a thousand. I might find some indifferent neutral-minded person who out of good nature or for a large sum of money would aid me in my bitter and desperate need. Certainly I would try to make what bargain I could now – now while I still had the strength to plead my cause and perhaps to extricate myself if the results were adverse. Still the odds were heavy against me, and it was with faltering and reluctant steps that I walked out of the shimmering gloom of the veldt into the light of the furnace fires, advanced towards the silent house, and struck with my fist upon the door.

There was a pause. Then I knocked again. And almost immediately a light sprang up above and an upper window opened.

'Wer ist da?' cried a man's voice.

I felt the shock of disappointment and consternation to my fingers.

'I want help; I have had an accident,' I replied.

Some muttering followed. Then I heard steps descending the stairs, the bolt of the door was drawn, the lock was turned. It was opened abruptly, and in the darkness of the passage a tall man hastily attired, with a pale face and dark moustache, stood before me.

'What do you want?' he said, this time in English.

I had now to think of something to say. I wanted above all to get into parley with this man, to get matters in such a state that instead of raising an alarm and summoning others he would discuss things quietly.

'I am a burgher,' I began. 'I have had an accident. I was going to join my commando at Komati Poort. I have fallen off the train. We were skylarking. I have been unconscious for hours. I think I have dislocated my shoulder.'

It is astonishing how one thinks of these things. This story leapt out as if I had learnt it by heart. Yet I had not the slightest idea what I was going to say or what the next sentence would be.

The stranger regarded me intently, and after some hesitation said at length, 'Well, come in.' He retreated a little into the darkness of the passage, threw open a door on one side of it, and pointed with his left hand into a dark room. I walked past him and entered, wondering if it was to be my prison. He followed, struck a light, lit a lamp, and set it on the table at the far side of which I stood. I was in a small room, evidently a dining-room and office in one. I noticed besides the large table, a roll desk, two or three chairs, and one of these machines for making soda-water, consisting of two glass globes set one above the other and encased in thin wire-netting. On his end of the table my host had laid a revolver, which he had hitherto presumably been holding in his right hand.

'I think I'd like to know a little more about this railway accident of yours,' he said, after a considerable pause.

'I think,' I replied, 'I had better tell you the truth.'

'I think you had,' he said slowly.

So I took the plunge and threw all I had upon the board. 'I am Winston Churchill, War Correspondent of the *Morning Post*. I escaped last night from Pretoria. I am making my way to the frontier.' (Making my way!) 'I have plenty of money. Will you help me?'

There was another long pause. My companion rose from the table slowly and locked the door. After this act, which struck me as unpromising, and was certainly ambiguous, he advanced upon me and suddenly held out his hand.

'Thank God you have come here! It is the only house for twenty miles where you would not have been handed over. But we are all British here, and we will see you through.'

It is easier to recall across the gulf of years the spasm of relief which swept over me, than it is to describe it. A moment before I had thought myself trapped; and now friends, food, resources, aid, were all at my disposal. I felt like a drowning man pulled out of the water and informed he had won the Derby!

My host now introduced himself as Mr John Howard, manager of the Transvaal Collieries. He had become a naturalized burgher of the Transvaal some years before the war. But out of consideration for his British race and some inducements which he had offered to the local Field Cornet, he had not been called up to fight against the British. Instead he had been allowed to remain with one or two others on the mine, keeping it pumped out and in good order until coal-cutting could be resumed. He had with him at the mine-head, besides his secretary, who was British, an engineman from Lancashire and two Scottish miners. All these four were British subjects and had been allowed to remain only upon giving their parole to observe strict neutrality. He himself as burgher of the Transvaal Republic would be guilty of treason in harbouring me, and liable to be shot if caught at the time or found out later on.

'Never mind,' he said, 'we will fix it up somehow.' And added, 'The Field Cornet was round here this afternoon asking about you. They had got the hue and cry out all along the line and all over the district.'

I said that I did not wish to compromise him.

Let him give me food, a pistol, a guide, and if possible a pony, and I would make my own way to the sea, marching by night across country far away from the railway line or any habitation.

He would not hear of it. He would fix up something. But he enjoined the utmost caution. Spies were everywhere. He had two Dutch servant-maids actually sleeping in the house. There were many Kaffirs employed about the mine premises and on the pumping-machinery of the mine. Surveying these dangers, he became very thoughtful.

Then : 'But you are famishing.'

I did not contradict him. In a moment he had bustled off into the kitchen, telling me meanwhile to help myself from a whisky bottle and the soda-water machine which I have already mentioned. He returned after an interval with the best part of a cold leg of mutton and various other delectable commodities, and, leaving me to do full justice to these, quitted the room and let himself out of the house by a back door.

Nearly an hour passed before Mr Howard returned. In this period my physical well-being had been brought into harmony with the improvement in my prospects. I felt confident of success and equal to anything.

'It's all right,' said Mr Howard. 'I have seen the men, and they are all for it. We must put you down the pit tonight, and there you will have to stay till we can see how to get you out of the country. One difficulty,' he said, 'will be the skoff (food). The Dutch girl sees every mouthful I eat. The cook will want to know what has happened to her leg of mutton. I shall have to think it all out during the night. You must get down the pit at once. We'll make you comfortable enough.'

Accordingly, just as the dawn was breaking, I followed my host across a little yard into the enclosure in which stood the winding-wheel of the mine. Here a stout man, introduced as Mr Dewsnap, of Oldham, locked my hand in a grip of crushing vigour.

'They'll all vote for you next time,' he whispered.

A door was opened and I entered the cage. Down we shot into the bowels of the earth. At the bottom of the mine were the two Scottish miners with lanterns and a big bundle which after-wards proved to be a mattress and blankets. We walked for some time through the pitchy labyrinth, with frequent turns, twists, and alterations of level, and finally stopped in a sort of chamber where the air was cool and fresh. Here my guide set down his bundle, and Mr Howard handed me a couple of candles, a bottle of whisky, and a box of cigars.

'There's no difficulty about these,' he said. 'I keep them under lock and key. Now we must plan how to feed you tomorrow.'

'Don't you move from here, whatever happens,' was the parting injunction. 'There will be Kaffirs about the mine after daylight, but we shall be on the look-out that none of them wanders this way. None of them has seen anything so far.'

My four friends trooped off with their lanterns, and I was left alone. Viewed from the velvety darkness of the pit, life seemed bathed in rosy light. After the perplexity and even despair through which I had passed I counted upon freedom as certain. Instead of a humiliating recapture and long months of monotonous imprisonment, probably in the common jail, I saw myself once more rejoining the Army with a real exploit to my credit, and in that full enjoyment of freedom and keen pursuit of adventure dear to the heart of youth. In this com-fortable mood, and speeded by intense fatigue, I soon slept the sleep of the weary – but of the triumphant.

I do not know how many hours I slept, but the following afternoon must have been far advanced when I found myself thoroughly awake. I put out my hand for the candle, but could feel it nowhere. I did not know what pitfalls these mining galleries might contain, so I thought it better to lie quiet on my mattress and await developments. Several hours passed before the faint gleam of a lantern showed that someone was coming. It proved to be Mr Howard himself, armed with a chicken and other good things. He also brought several books. He asked me why I had not lighted my candle. I said I couldn't find it.

'Didn't you put it under the mattress?' he asked.

'No.'

'Then the rats must have got it.'

He told me there were swarms of rats in the mines, that some years ago he had introduced a particular kind of white rat, which was an excellent scavenger, and that these had multiplied exceedingly. He told me he had been to the house of an English doctor twenty miles away to get the chicken. He was worried at the attitude of the two Dutch servants, who were very inquisitive about the depredations upon the leg of mutton for which I had been responsible. If he could not get another chicken cooked for the next day, he would have to take double helpings on his own plate and slip the surplus into a parcel for me while the servant was out of the room. He said that inquiries were being made for me all over the district by the Boers, and that the Pretoria Government was making a tremendous fuss about my escape. The fact that there were a number of English remaining in the Middleburg mining region indicated it as a likely place for me to have turned to, and all persons of English origin were more or less suspect.

I again expressed my willingness to go on alone with a Kaffir guide and a pony, but this he utterly refused to entertain. It would take a lot of planning, he said, to get me out of the country, and I might have to stay in the mine for quite a long time.

'Here,' he said, 'you are absolutely safe. Mac' (by which he meant one of the Scottish miners) 'knows all the disused workings and places that no one else would dream of. There is one place here where the water actually touches the roof for a foot or two. If they searched the mine, Mac would dive under that with you into the workings cut off beyond the water. No one would ever think of looking there. We have frightened the Kaffirs with tales of ghosts, and anyhow, we are watching their movements, continually.'

He stayed with me while I dined, and then departed, leaving me, among other things, half a dozen candles which, duly warned, I tucked under my pillow and mattress.

I slept again for a long time, and woke suddenly with a feeling of movement about me. Something seemed to be pulling at my pillow. I put out my hand quickly. There was a perfect scurry. The rats were at the candles. I rescued the candles in time, and lighted one. Luckily for me, I have no horror of rats as such, and being reassured by their evident timidity, I was not particularly uneasy. All the same, the three days I passed in the mine were not among the most pleasant which my memory re-illumines. The patter of little feet and a perceptible sense of stir and scurry were continous. Once I was waked up from a doze by one actually galloping across me. On the candle being lighted these beings became invisible.

The next day – if you can call it day – arrived in due course. This was December 14, and the third day since I had escaped from the State Model Schools. It was relieved by a visit from the two Scottish miners, with whom I had a long confabulation. I then learned, to my surprise, that the mine was only about two hundred feet deep.

There were parts of it, said Mac, where one could see the daylight up a disused shaft. Would I like to take a turn around the old workings and have a glimmer? We passed an hour or two wandering round and up and down these subterranean galleries, and spent a quarter of an hour near the bottom of the shaft, where, grey and faint, the light of the sun and of the upper world was discerned. On this promenade I saw numbers of rats. They seemed rather nice little beasts, quite white, with dark eyes which I was assured in the daylight were a bright pink. Three years afterwards a British officer on duty in the district wrote to me that he had heard my statement at a lecture about the white rats and their pink eyes, and thought it was the limit of mendacity. He had taken the trouble to visit the mine and see for himself, and he proceeded to apologize for having doubted my truthfulness.

On the 15th Mr Howard announced that the hue and cry seemed to be dying away. No trace of the fugitive had been discovered throughout the mining district. The talk among the Boer officials was now that I must be hiding at the house of some British sympathizer in Pretoria. They did not believe that it was possible I could have got out of the town. In these circumstances he thought that I might come up and have a walk on the veldt that night, and that if all was quiet the next morning I might shift my quarters to the back room of the office. On the one hand he seemed reassured, and on the other increasingly excited by the adventure. Accordingly, I had a fine stroll in the glorious fresh air and moonlight, and thereafter, anticipating slightly our programme, I took up my quarters behind packing-cases in the inner room of the office. Here I remained for three more days, walking each night on the endless plain with Mr Howard or his assistant.

On the 16th, the fifth day of escape, Mr Howard informed me he had made a plan to get me out of the country. The mine was connected with the railway by a branch line. In the neighbourhood of the mine there lived a Dutchman, Burgener by name, who was sending a consignment of wool to Delagoa Bay on the 19th. This gentleman was well disposed to the British. He had been approached by Mr Howard, had been made a party to our secret, and was willing to assist. Mr Burgener's wool was packed in great bales and would fill two or three large trucks. These trucks were to be loaded at the mine's siding. The bales could be so packed as to leave a small place in the centre of the truck in which I could be concealed. A tarpaulin would be fastened over each truck after it had been loaded, and it was very unlikely that, if the fastenings were found intact, it would be removed at the frontier. Did I agree to take this chance?

I was more worried about this than almost anything that had happened to me so far in my adventure. When by extraordinary chance one has gained some great advantage or prize and actually had it in one's possession and been enjoying it for several days, the idea of losing it becomes almost insupportable. I had really come to count upon freedom as a certainty, and the idea of having to put myself in a position in which I should be perfectly helpless, without a move of any kind, absolutely at the caprice of a searching party at the frontier, was profoundly harassing. Rather than face this ordeal I would much have preferred to start off on the veldt with a pony and a guide, and far from the haunts of man to make my way march by march beyond the wide territories of the Boer Republic. However, in the end I accepted the proposal of my generous rescuer, and arrangements were made accordingly.

I should have been still more anxious if I could have read

some of the telegrams which were reaching English news-papers. For instance.

*Pretoria, December 13.* – Though Mr Churchill's escape was clev-erly executed there is little chance of his being able to cross the border.

*Pretoria, December 14.* – It is reported that Mr Winston Churchill has been captured at the border railway station of Komati Poort.

*Lourenco Marques, December 16.* – It is reported that Mr Churchill has been captured at Waterval Boven.

*London, December 16.* – With reference to the escape from Pretoria of Mr Winston Churchill, fears are expressed that he may be captured again before long and if so may probably be shot;

or if I had read the description of myself and the reward for my recapture which were now widely distributed or posted along the railway line (wording of which is given on the next page).

I am glad I knew nothing of all this.

The afternoon of the 18th dragged slowly away. I remember that I spent the greater part of it reading Stevenson's *Kidnapped*. Those thrilling pages which describe the escape of David Balfour and Alan Breck in the glens awakened sensations with which I was only too familiar. To be a fugitive, to be a hunted man, to be 'wanted', is a mental experience by itself. The risks of the battlefield, the hazards of the bullet or the shell are one thing. Having the police after you is another. The need for concealment and deception breeds an actual sense of guilt very undermining to morale. Feeling that at any moment the officers of the law may present themselves or any stranger may ask the questions, 'Who are you?' 'Where do you come from?' 'Where are you going?' – to which questions no satisfactory answer could be given – gnawed the structure of self-confidence. I dreaded in every fibre the ordeal which awaited me at Komati Poort and which I must impotently and passively endure if I was to make good my escape from the enemy.

In this mood I was startled by the sound of rifle-shots close at hand, one after another at irregular intervals. A sinister

# £25
# REWARD

(Twenty-five Pounds stg.) RE-
WARD is offered by the Sub-
Commission of the fifth division,
on behalf of the Special Consta-
ble of the said division, to anyone who brings the escaped
prisoner of war

# CHURCHILL

*Dead or Alive to this office*
For the Sub-Commission of
the fifth division.
*(signed)* LODK. de HASS, Sec.

explanation flashed through my mind. The Boers had come! Howard and his handful of Englishmen were in open rebellion in the heart of the enemy's country! I had been strictly enjoined upon no account to leave my hiding-place behind the packing-cases in any circumstances whatever, and I accordingly remained there in great anxiety. Presently it became clear that the worst had not happened. The sounds of voices and presently laughter came from the office. Evidently a conversation amicable, sociable in its character was in progress. I resumed my companionship with Alan Breck. At last the voices died away, and then after an interval my door was opened and Mr Howard's pale, sombre face appeared, suffused by a broad grin. He unlocked the door behind him and walked delicately towards me, evidently in high glee.

'The Field Cornet has been here,' he said. 'No, he was not looking for you. He says they caught you at Waterval Boven yesterday. But I didn't want him messing about, so I challenged him to a rifle match at bottles. He won two pounds off me and has gone away delighted.'

'It is all fixed up for tonight,' he added.

'What do I do?' I asked.

'Nothing. You simply follow me when I come for you.'

At two o'clock on the morning of the 19th I awaited, fully dressed, the signal. The door opened. My host appeared. He beckoned. Not a word was spoken on either side. He led the way through the front office to the siding where three large bogie trucks stood. Three figures evidently Dewsnap and the miners, were strolling about in different directions in the moonlight. A gang of Kaffirs were busy lifting an enormous bale into the nearmost truck. Howard strolled along to the first truck and walked across the line past the end of it. As he did so he pointed with his left hand. I nipped on to the buffers and saw before me a hole between the wool bales and the end of the truck, just wide enough to squeeze into. From this there led a narrow tunnel formed of wool bales into the centre of the truck. Here was a space wide enough to lie in, high enough to sit up in. In this I took up my abode.

Three or four hours later, when gleams of daylight had reached me through the interstices of my shelter and through chinks in the boards of the flooring of the truck, the noise of an approaching engine was heard. Then came the bumping and banging of coupling-up. And again, after a further pause, we started rumbling off on our journey into the unknown.

I now took stock of my new abode and of the resources in munitions and supplies with which it was furnished. First there was a revolver. This was a moral support, though it was not easy to see in what way it could helpfully be applied to any problem I was likely to have to solve. Secondly, there were two roast chickens, some slices of meat, a loaf of bread, a melon, and three bottles of cold tea. The journey to the sea was not expected to take more than sixteen hours, but no one could tell what delay might occur to ordinary commercial traffic in time of war.

There was plenty of light now in the recess in which I was confined. There were many crevices in the boards composing the sides and floor of the truck, and through these the light found its way between the wool bales. Working along the tunnel to the end of the truck, I found a chink which must have been nearly an eighth of an inch in width, and through which it was possible to gain a partial view of the outer world. To check the progress of the journey I had learnt by heart beforehand the names of all the stations on the route. I can remember many of them today: Witbank, Middleburg, Bergendal, Belfast, Dalmanutha, Machadodorp, Waterval Boven, Waterval Ondet, Elands, Nooidgedacht, and so on to Komati Poort. We had by now reached the first of these. At this point the branch line from the mine joined the railway. Here, after two or three hours' delay and shunting, we were evidently coupled up to a regular train, and soon started off at a superior and very satisfactory pace.

All day long we travelled eastward through the Transvaal; when darkness fell we were laid up for the night at a station which, according to my reckoning, was Waterval Boven. We had accomplished nearly half of our journey. But how long should we wait on this siding? It might be for days; it would certainly be until the next morning. During all the dragging hours of the day I had lain on the floor of the truck occupying my mind as best I could, painting bright pictures of the pleasure of freedom, of the excitement of rejoining the Army, of the triumph of a successful escape – but haunted also perpetually by anxieties about the search at the frontier, an ordeal inevitable and constantly approaching. Now another apprehension laid hold upon me. I wanted to go to sleep. Indeed, I did not think I could possibly keep awake. But if I slept I might snore! And if I snored while the train was at rest in the silent siding, I might be heard. And if I were heard! I decided in principle that it was only prudent to abstain from sleep, and shortly afterwards fell into blissful slumber from which I was awakened the next morning by the banging and jerking of the train as the engine was again coupled to it.

Between Waterval Boven and Waterval Onder there is a very steep descent which the locomotive accomplishes by means of a rack and pinion. We ground our way down this at three or four miles an hour, and this feature made my reckoning certain that the next station was, in fact, Waterval Onder. All this day, too, we rattled through the enemy's country, and late in the afternoon we reached the dreaded Komati Poort. Peeping through my chink, I could see this was a considerable place, with numerous tracks of rails and several trains standing on them. Numbers of people were moving about. There were many voices and much shouting and whistling. After a preliminary inspection of the scene I retreated, as the train pulled up, into the very centre of my fastness, and covering myself up with a piece of sacking lay flat on the floor of the truck and awaited developments with a beating heart.

Three or four hours passed, and I did not know whether we had been searched or not. Several times people had passed up and down the train talking in Dutch. But the tarpaulins had not been removed, and no special examination seemed to have been made of the truck. Meanwhile darkness had come on, and I had to resign myself to an indefinite continuance of my uncertainties. It was tantalizing to be held so long in jeopardy after all these hundreds of miles had been accomplished, and

I was now within a few hundred yards of the frontier. Again I wondered about the dangers of snoring. But in the end I slept without mishap.

We were still stationary when I awoke. Perhaps they were searching the train so thoroughly that there was consequently a great delay! Alternatively, perhaps we were forgotten on the siding and would be left there for days or weeks. I was greatly tempted to peer out, but I resisted. At last, at eleven o'clock, we were coupled up, and almost immediately started. If I had been right in thinking that the station in which we had passed the night was Komati Poort, I was already in Portuguese territory. But perhaps I had made a mistake. Perhaps I had miscounted. Perhaps there was still another station before the frontier. Perhaps the search still impended. But all these doubts were dispelled when the train arrived at the next station. I peered through my chink and saw the uniform of the Portuguese officials on the platform and the name Resana Garcia painted on a board. I restrained all expression of my joy until we moved on again. Then, as we rumbled and banged along, I pushed my head out of the tarpaulin and sang and shouted at the top of my voice. Indeed, I was so carried away by thankfulness and delight that I fired my revolver two or three times in the air as a feu de joie. None of these follies led to any evil results.

It was late in the afternoon when we reached Lourenco Marques. My train ran into a goods yard, and a crowd of Kaffirs advanced to unload it. I thought the moment had now come for me to quit my hiding-place, in which I had passed nearly three anxious and uncomfortable days. I had already thrown out every vestige of food and had removed all traces of my occupation. I now slipped out at the end of the truck between the couplings, and mingling unnoticed with the Kaffirs and loafers in the yard – which my slovenly and unkempt appearance well fitted me to do – I strolled my way towards the gates and found myself in the streets of Lourenco Marques.

Burgener was waiting outside the gates. We exchanged glances. He turned and walked off into the town, and I followed twenty yards behind. We walked through several streets and turned a number of corners. Presently he stopped and stood for a moment gazing up at the roof of the opposite house. I looked in the same direction, and there – blest vision! – I saw floating the gay colours of the Union Jack. It was the British Consulate.

The secretary of the British Consul evidently did not expect my arrival.

'Be off,' he said. 'The Consul cannot see you today. Come to his office at nine tomorrow, if you want anything.'

At this I became so angry, and repeated so loudly that I insisted on seeing the Consul personally at once, that that gentleman himself looked out of the window and finally came down to the door and asked me my name. From that moment every resource of hospitality and welcome was at my disposal. A hot bath, clean clothing, an excellent dinner, means of tele-graphing – all I could want.

I devoured the file of newspapers which was placed before me. Great events had taken place since I had climbed the wall of the State Model Schools. The Black Week of the Boer War had descended on the British Army. General Gatacre at Storm-berg, Lord Methuen at Magersfontein, and Sir Redvers Buller at Colenso, had all suffered staggering defeats, and casualties on a scale unknown to England since the Crimean War. All this made me eager to rejoin the Army, and the Consul himself was no less anxious to get me out of Lourenco Marques, which was full of Boers and Boer sympathizers. Happily the weekly steamer was leaving for Durban that very evening; in fact, it might almost be said it ran in connection with my train. On this steamer I decided to embark.

The news of my arrival had spread like wildfire through the town, and while we were at dinner the Consul was at first disturbed to see a group of strange figures in the garden. These, however, turned out to be Englishmen fully armed who had hurried up to the Consulate determined to resist any attempt at my recapture. Under the escort of these patriotic gentlemen I marched safely through the streets to the quay, and at about ten o'clock was on salt water in the steam ship *Induna*.

I reached Durban to find myself a popular hero. I was received as if I had won a great victory. The harbour was decorated with flags. Bands and crowds thronged the quays. The Admiral, the General, the Mayor pressed on board to grasp my hand. I was nearly torn to pieces by enthusiastic kindness. Whirled along on the shoulders of the crowd, I was carried to the steps of the town hall, where nothing would content them but a speech, which after a becoming reluctance I was induced to deliver. Sheaves of telegrams from all parts of the world poured in upon me, and I started that night for the Army in a blaze of triumph.

Here, too, I was received with the greatest goodwill. I took up my quarters in the very platelayer's hut within one hundred yards of which I had a little more than a month before been taken prisoner, and there with the rude plenty of the Natal campaign celebrated by a dinner to many friends my good fortune and Christmas Eve.

– from *My Early Life*

EDWARD WHYMPER

# Escape from the Matterhorn

Many climbers can tell stories of escapes from mountains, in storms or after accidents. This escape was one of the first, and one of the most controversial: for years after it, the men who escaped were suspected of having cut the rope when the crisis came.

Edward Whymper, who wrote this account, had been planning for years to be the first man to climb the Matterhorn. Just before he started, from Zermatt on the Swiss side of the mountain, he heard that a party of Italians was about to try it from the other side. He determined to beat them to the top. Three fellow Englishmen and four Swiss guides went with him.

We started from Zermatt on the 13th of July 1865, at half-past five, on a brilliant and perfectly cloudless morning. We were eight in number – Croz, old Peter Taugwalder and his two sons, Lord F. Douglas, Hadow, Hudson, and I. To ensure steady motion, one tourist and one native walked together. The youngest Taugwalder fell to my share, and the lad marched well, proud to be on the expedition, and happy to show his powers. The wine-bags also fell to my lot to carry, and throughout the day, after each drink, I replenished them with water, so that at the next halt they were found fuller than before! This was considered a good omen, and little short of miraculous.

On the first day we did not intend to ascend to any great height, and we mounted, accordingly, very leisurely; picked up the things which were left in the chapel at the Schwarzse at 8.20, and proceeded thence along the ridge connecting the Hornli with the Matterhorn. At half-past eleven we arrived at the base of the actual peak; then quitted the ridge, and clambered round some ledges on to the eastern face. We were now fairly upon the mountain, and were astonished to find that places which from the Riffel, or even from the Furggengletscher, looked entirely impracticable, were so easy that we could run about.

Before twelve o'clock we had found a good position for the tent, at a height of 11,000 feet. Croz and young Peter went on to see what was above, in order to save time on the following morning. They cut across the heads of the snow-slopes which descended towards the Furggengletscher, and disappeared round a corner; but shortly afterwards we saw them both high up on the face, moving quickly. We others made a solid platform for the tent in a well-protected spot, and then watched eagerly for the return of the men. The stones which they upset told us that they were very high, and we supposed that the way must be easy. At length, just before 3 p.m., we saw them coming down, evidently much excited. 'What are they saying, Peter?' 'Gentlemen, they say it is no good.' But when they came near we heard a different story. 'Nothing but what was good; not a difficulty, not a single difficulty! We could have gone to the summit and returned today easily!'

We passed the remaining hours of daylight – some basking in the sunshine, some sketching or collecting; and when the sun went down, giving as it departed, a glorious promise for the morrow, we returned to the tent to arrange for the night. Hudson made tea, I coffee, and we then retired each one to his blanket-bag – the Taugwalders, Lord Francis Douglas, and myself occupying the tent; the others remaining, by preference, outside. Long after dusk the cliffs above echoed with our laughter and with the songs of the guides; for we were happy that night in camp, and feared no evil.

We assembled together outside the tent before dawn on the morning of the 14th, and started directly it was light enough to move. Young Peter came on with us as a guide, and his brother returned to Zermatt. We followed the route which had been taken on the previous day, and in a few minutes turned the rib which had intercepted the view of the eastern face from our tent platform. The whole of this great slope was now revealed, rising for 3,000 feet like a huge natural staircase. Some parts were more and others were less easy; but we were not once brought to a halt by any serious impediment, for when an obstruction was met in front it could always be turned to the right or to the left. For the greater part of the way there was, indeed, no occasion for the rope, and sometimes Hudson led, sometimes myself. At 6.20 we had attained a height of 12,800 feet, and halted for half an hour; we then continued the ascent without a break until 9.55, when we stopped for fifty minutes, at a height of 14,000 feet. Twice we struck the N.E. ridge and followed it for some little distance – to no advantage, for it was usually more rotten and steep, and always more difficult than the face. Still, we kept near to it, lest stones perchance might fall.

We had now arrived at the foot of that part which, from the Riffelberg, or from Zermatt, seems perpendicular or over-hanging, and could no longer continue upon the eastern side. For a little distance we ascended by snow upon the arête – that is, the ridge – descending towards Zermatt, and then, by common consent, turned over to the right, or to the northern side. Before doing so, we made a change in the order of ascent. Croz went first, I followed, Hudson came third; Hadow and old Peter were last. 'Now,' said Croz, as he led off – 'now for something altogether different.' The work became difficult, and required caution. In some places there was little hold, and it was desirable that those should be in front who were least likely to slip. The general slope of the mountain at this part was less than 40°, and snow had accumulated in, and had filled up, the interstices of the rock face, leaving only occasional fragments projecting here and there. These were at times covered with a thin film of ice, produced from the melting and refreezing of the snow. It was the counterpart, on a small scale, of the upper 700 feet of the Points des Ecrins; only there was this material difference – the face of the Ecrins was about, or exceeded, an angle of 50°, and the Matterhorn face was less than 40°. It was a place over which any fair mountaineer might pass in safety, and Mr Hudson ascended this part, and, as far as I know, the entire mountain, without having the slightest assistance rendered to him upon any occasion. Sometimes, after I had taken a hand from Croz, or received a pull, I turned to offer the same to Hudson; but he invariably declined, saying it was not necessary. Mr Hadow, however, was not accustomed to this kind of work, and required continual assistance. It is only fair to say that the difficulty which he found at this part arose simply and entirely from want of experience.

The solitary difficult part was of no great extent. We bore away over it at first, nearly horizontally, for a distance of about 400 feet; then ascended directly towards the summit for about 60 feet; and then doubled back to the ridge which descends towards Zermatt. A long stride round a rather awkward corner brought us to snow once more. The last doubt vanished! The Matterhorn was ours! Nothing but 200 feet of easy snow remained to be surmounted!

You must now carry your thoughts back to the seven Italians who started from Breuil on the 11th of July. Four days had passed since their departure, and we were tormented with anxiety lest they should arrive on the top before us. All the way up we had talked of them, and many false alarms of 'men on the summit' had been raised. The higher we rose, the more intense became the excitement. What if we should be beaten at the last moment? The slope eased off, at length we could be detached, and Croz and I, dashing away, ran a neck-and-neck race, which ended in a dead heat. At 1.40 p.m. the world was at our feet, and the Matterhorn was conquered. Hurrah! Not a footstep could be seen.

It was not yet certain that we had not been beaten. The summit of the Matterhorn was formed of a rudely level ridge, about 350 feet long, and the Italians might have been at its farther extremity. I hastened to the southern end, scanning the snow right and left eagerly. Hurrah again – it was untrodden! 'Where were the men?' I peered over the cliff, half doubting, half expectant, and saw them immediately – mere dots on the ridge, at an immense distance below. Up went my arms and my hat. 'Croz! Croz! come here!' 'Where are they, Monsieur?' 'There – don't you see them – down there!' 'Ah! the coquins, they are low down.' 'Croz we must make those fellows hear us.' We yelled until we were hoarse. The Italians seemed to regard us – we could not be certain. 'Croz, we must make them hear us; they shall hear us!' I seized a block of rock and hurled it down, and called upon my companion, in the name of friendship, to do the same. We drove our sticks in, and prized away the crags, and soon a torrent of stones poured down the cliffs. There was no mistake about it this time. The Italians turned and fled.

Still I would that the leader of that party could have stood with us at that moment, for our victorious shouts conveyed to him the disappointment of the ambition of a lifetime. He was the man, of all those who attempted the ascent of the Matterhorn, who most deserved to be the first upon its summit. He was the first to doubt its inaccessibility, and he was the only man who persisted in believing that its ascent would be accomplished. It was the aim of his life to make the ascent from the side of Italy, for the honour of his native valley. For a time he had the game in his hands: he played it as he thought best; but he made a false move, and he lost it.

The others had arrived, so we went back to the northern end of the ridge. Croz now took the tent-pole, and planted it in the highest snow. 'Yes,' we said, 'there is the flagstaff, but where is the flag?' 'Here it is,' he answered, pulling off his blouse and fixing it to the stick. It made a poor flag, and there was no wind to float it out, yet it was seen all around. They saw it at Zermatt – at the Riffel – in the Val Tournanche. At Breuil the watchers cried, 'Victory is ours!' They raised 'bravos' for Carrel and 'vivas' for Italy, and hastened to put themselves *en fête*. On the morrow they were undeceived. 'All was changed; the explorers returned sad – cast down – disheartened – confounded – gloomy.' 'It is true,' said the men. 'We saw them ourselves – they hurled stones at us! The old traditions are true – there are spirits on the top of the Matterhorn!'

Hudson and I again consulted as to the best and safest arrangement of the party. We agreed that it would be best for Croz to go first, and Hadow second; Hudson, who was almost equal to a born mountaineer in sureness of foot, wished to be third; Lord Francis Douglas was placed next; and old Peter, the strongest of the remainder, after him. I suggested to Hudson that we should attach a rope to the rocks on our arrival at the difficult bit, and hold it as we descended, as an additional protection. He approved the idea, but it was not definitely settled that it should be done. The party was being arranged in the above order whilst I was sketching the summit, and they had finished, and were waiting for me to be tied in line, when someone remembered that our names had not been left in a bottle. They requested me to write them down, and moved off while it was being done.

A few minutes afterwards I tied myself to young Peter, ran down after the others, and caught them just as they were commencing the descent of the difficult part. Great care was being taken. Only one man was moving at a time: when he was firmly planted the next advanced, and so on. They had not, however, attached the additional rope to rocks, and nothing was said about it. The suggestion was not made for my own sake, and I am not sure that it even occurred to me again. For some little distance we two followed the others, detached from them, and should have continued so had not Lord Francis Douglas asked me, about 3 p.m. to tie on to old Peter, as he feared, he said, that Taugwalder would not be able to hold his ground if a slip occurred.

A few minutes later a sharp-eyed lad ran into the Monte Rosa hotel, to Seiler, saying that he had seen an avalanche fall from the summit of the Matterhorn on to the Matterhorn-gletscher. The boy was reproved for telling idle stories; he was right, nevertheless, and this was what he saw.

Michel Croz had laid aside his axe, and in order to give Mr Hadow greater security, was absolutely taking hold of his legs, and putting his feet, one by one, into their proper positions. So far as I know, no one was actually descending. I cannot speak with certainty, because the two leading men were partially hidden from my sight by an intervening mass of rocks, but it is my belief, from the movements of their shoulders, that Croz, having done as I have said, was in the act of turning round, to go down a step or two himself; at this moment Mr Hadow slipped, fell against him, and knocked him over. I heard one startled exclamation from Croz, then saw him and Mr Hadow flying downwards; in another moment Hudson was dragged from his steps, and Lord F. Douglas immediately after him. All this was the work of a moment. Immediately we heard Croz's exclamation, old Peter and I planted ourselves as firmly as the rocks would permit: the rope was taut between us, and the jerk came on both of us as on one man. We held; but the rope broke midway between Taugwalder and Lord Francis Douglas. For a few seconds we saw our unfortunate companions sliding downwards on their backs, and spreading out their hands, endeavouring to save themselves. They passed from our sight uninjured, disappeared one by one, and fell from precipice to precipice on to the Matterhorngletscher below, a distance of nearly 4,000 feet in height. From the moment the rope broke it was impossible to help them.

So perished our comrades! For the space of half an hour we remained on the spot without moving a single step. The two men, paralysed by terror, cried like infants, and trembled in such a manner as to threaten us with the fate of the others. Old Peter rent the air with exclamations of 'Chamounix! Oh, what will Chamounix say?' He meant, Who would believe that Croz could fall? The young man did nothing but scream or sob, 'We are lost! We are lost!' Fixed between the two, I could neither move up nor down. I begged young Peter to descend, but he dared not. Unless he did we could not advance. Old Peter became alive to the danger, and swelled the cry, 'We are lost! We are lost!' The father's fear was natural – he trembled for his son; the young man's fear was cowardly – he thought of self alone. At last old Peter summoned up courage, and changed his position to a rock to which he could fix the rope; the young man then descended, and we all stood together. Immediately we did so I asked for the rope which had given way, and found, to my surprise – indeed to my horror – that it was the weakest of the three ropes. It was not brought, and should not have been employed, for the purpose for which it was used. It was old rope, and, compared with the others, was feeble. It was intended as a reserve, in case we had to leave much rope behind, attached to rocks. I saw at once that a serious question was involved, and made him give me the end. It had broken in mid-air, and it did not appear to have sustained previous injury.

For more than two hours afterwards I thought almost every moment that the next would be my last; for the Taugwalders, utterly unnerved, were not only incapable of giving assistance, but were in such a state that a slip might have been expected from them at any moment. After a time we were able to do that which should have been done at first, and fixed rope to firm rocks, in addition to being tied together. These ropes were cut from time to time, and were left behind. Even with their assurance the men were afraid to proceed, several times old Peter turned with ashy face and faltering limbs, and said, with terrible emphasis, 'I cannot!'

About 6 p.m. we arrived at the snow upon the ridge descending towards Zermatt, and all peril was over. We frequently looked, but in vain, for traces of our unfortunate companions; we bent over the ridge and cried to them, but no sound returned. Convinced at last that they were neither within sight nor hearing, we ceased from our useless efforts, and too cast down for speech, silently gathered up our things, and the little effects of those who were lost, preparatory to continuing the descent; when, lo! a mighty arch appeared, rising above the Lyskamm, high into the sky. Pale, colourless, and noiseless, but perfectly sharp and defined, except where it was lost in the clouds, this unearthly apparition seemed like a vision from another world; and, almost appalled, we watched with amazement the gradual development of two vast crosses, one on either side. If the Taugwalders had not been the first to perceive it, I should have doubted my senses. They thought it had some connection with the accident, and I, after a while, that it might bear some relation to ourselves. But our movements had no effect upon it. The spectral forms remained motionless. It was a fearful and wonderful sight; unique in my experience, and impressive beyond description, coming at such a moment.

Night fell, and for an hour the descent was continued in the darkness. At half-past nine a resting-place was found, and upon a wretched slab, barely large enough to hold the three, we passed six miserable hours. At daybreak the descent was resumed, and from the Hornli ridge we ran down to the chalets of Buh, and on to Zermatt.

– from *Scrambles Amongst the Alps*

ALAN BURGESS

# A Hundred Chinese Children

Gladys Aylward was a servant in a large London house. In 1930, she decided to become a missionary in China. She was very small, very poor and little educated, but she had great determination, and she travelled alone to a distant part of China. Many years later, she was still working there and was looking after a hundred orphan children. The Japanese invaded China and the part where she lived became a battlefield. She had to escape – with her children.

At sun-up the young children were up and shouting, running round the courtyard, throwing their bundles of bedding at each other, playing 'Tag' and generally behaving in the normal way of young children all over the world. With the aid of the older ones, Gladys tried to sort them out and feed them. There were nearly twenty big girls, ages varying from thirteen to fifteen, Ninepence and Sualan amongst them : there were seven big boys aged between eleven and fifteen; the rest of the children varied from four to eight, wild undisciplined, laughing, weeping, shouting little brats. In vain, she tried to tell them that they must save their energy for the long day ahead; she might just as usefully have told a stream to stop running. The two coolies from Mandarin, carrying their shoulder-poles, a basket of millet suspended at either end, arrived at the front gate. Gladys said good-bye to the two Mission workers, to several other friends collected there; and, after one last look round the broken Inn, they were on their way, the children scampering ahead, dodging back through the gates of the city, shouting loudly that they could walk for ever and ever.

They followed the main trail southwards for several miles. Gladys possessed a whistle which she had obtained from a Japanese soldier months before, and she blew it occasionally to call the more adventurous little boys down from outcrops of rocks, and twice to line them all up in rows for a roll call to see that no one was missing.

They stopped by a stream to boil millet in the iron pot which Gladys carried; she heaped the steaming grain into the basins as each child came up in turn for its helping. At the end of this serving there wasn't much left in the pot for her, and from that moment onwards that was the way things usually turned out. The children, revived after the meal, began to clamber about the rocks again, and made excited forays ahead, to lie in wait and ambush the main party. She gave up trying to keep them in order, but as the afternoon progressed, these minor expeditions became fewer and fewer, and soon she had four small ones hanging on to her coat, protesting that they were tired, and could they all go back to Yangcheng now? Gladys took it in turns with the older boys to carry them. She felt a little tired herself.

It was getting dark when they came to a mountain village she knew, and where she thought they might find shelter for the night. Not, she thought, that any householders would be particularly anxious to house a hundred noisy, dirty children. Help came from an unexpected quarter. An old Buddhist priest, in his bright saffron robes, stood on the steps of his temple as the Pied Piper of Yangcheng and her brood straggled past.

'Where are you going?' he called to Gladys.

'We are refugees on the way to Sian,' she said.

He came down the steps and approached her, his small eyes almost lost in the maze of wrinkles and lines that creased his face.

'But what are you going to do with all these children, woman?' He sounded most disapproving.

'I'm looking for a place for us to sleep tonight.'

'Then you can stay in the temple,' he said abruptly. 'All my brother priests are away. There is plenty of room. Tell them to come in. It will be warmer than the mountainside.'

The children needed no prompting. This was something like an adventure! It was dark in the temple, and there were gloomy recesses in which stone figures of the fat, bland, heavy-lidded Buddha resided. There were pointed panels depicting the many tortures of sinners, but the children were too tired to notice them. They crowded round the iron pot when Gladys had finished cooking the millet, and when they had eaten, they curled up on their bedding and went fast asleep.

She did not sleep so easily. For one thing, the temple was alive with rats, who twittered in the darkness and ran over the sleeping children; and a small creeping doubt had entered her mind concerning the wisdom of starting this journey with so many small ones. Perhaps she was over-estimating her own ability? It was one thing to journey through the mountains alone; quite another to take a hundred children with you. The first day had been troublesome enough, yet all the children were fresh, and she was crossing country she knew intimately. The older girls had not complained, but she could see that several of them had suffered already. They were completely unused to mountain walking; the feet of several of them had once been bound, and even many years free from the bindings were insufficient to turn them into healthy limbs able to withstand the drag and scrape of the rocky paths. For perhaps an hour the big boys tried to keep off the rats, then they also became too tired to persevere and fell asleep. Gladys lay on the hard floor; above her head the impassive sculptured face of the stone Buddha was illumined by a shaft of moonlight streaming downwards through some aperture high above. The more she thought about the future, the less she liked it, but there was no chance of retreat now; she had to go on.

The next day was a replica of the first. The children awoke refreshed, and with a complete lack of reverence began to explore the temple with shrill, admiring cries. The priest smiled urbanely; he did not seem to mind at all. He bowed when Gladys offered her thanks and wished her a safe journey to Sian.

They were far from any village when the next night caught them, and they huddled together in the shelter of a semi-circle of rocks out of the wind. In the night there was a heavy mist and the children crept under their wet quilts, and next day they steamed and dried out when the sun rose. That afternoon they met a man on a mule travelling in the same direction as themselves. If they would come to his village, he said, he would be glad to find them shelter for the night. She accepted his offer gratefully. In his courtyard the children spread themselves out

and scooped cooked millet out of their bowls until their bellies
were full, then drank cupful after cupful of the hot twig tea.
They still thought it was all a wonderful adventure. Even Gladys
felt an immense sense of relief with another day safely past,
and the Yellow River one day closer. She cupped her bowl between her hands, embracing the tiny warmth it offered, and
chatted to the other girls.

'How many days will it take us to reach the Yellow River,
Ai-weh-deh?' asked Sualan diffidently.

Although Gladys had never been through to the Yellow River,
she knew the answer to that question without any trouble. 'The
muleteers on the normal track used to take five days. We're
going right through the mountains. About twelve, I'd say.'

'And we shan't see a single Japanese soldier the whole way?'
asked Ninepence.

'I hope not,' she answered.

She looked at the two girls as they chatted, the girl she had
bought for ninepence, and the slave girl from the Yamen. They
were both exquisite creatures with clear pale skins and blue-
black shining hair. Even in their dusty padded coats their pretti-
ness was still unimpaired. She thought wistfully how beautiful
they would look in the ceremonial robes of China, wondering
if they would ever know such luxury. How absurd that they
should be forced to make this long journey to save their lives.
She felt an unreasoning anger at the stupidity of all men that
they should be the cause of this ordeal. She yawned. It was odd,
this constant tiredness. 'Probably the added responsibility of
the children,' she thought to herself, as she wrapped herself in
her bedding quilt and lay down to sleep.

In the morning the two carriers of the millet had to return
to Yangcheng. They had reached the limit of their province.
However, the man they had met in the mountains proved a
good friend; he provided them with another coolie who would
carry what was left of the millet until it was finished, and even
by rationing it did not look as if that would last another two
days.

The next two nights were spent in the open. Two of the older
boys, Teh and Liang, had obtained a pot of whitewash from a

village along the way, and they went on ahead daubing a splash of white on to the rocks to mark the trail across the mountains. Sometimes they would write a text across a rock : *This is the way. Walk ye in it!* or *Fear ye not, little flock!* There were squeals of appreciation as the messages were translated to the young ones.

This was new country to Gladys, but she knew they were heading south by the direction of the sun. They were thirsty practically all the time, for the sun was hot and wells were only to be found in the villages. After the heavy wet mountain mists each morning they would gather round any drip from the rocks and moisten their tongues. The millet was used up now, and the carrier went back to his village. They had no more food, and the mountain stretched ahead of them, wild and barren, with few places of habitation. Often, when they climbed over virgin rock, the slopes were so steep that they had to form a human chain down the mountainside, and pass the younger children down from hand to hand. They cried when they fell down, and cried when they got tired. Often Gladys tried to rally them with a hymn, and when they reached a level patch of ground they would all march bravely along singing the chorus. Between them, the older children and Gladys were carrying practically all the bedding now, and often they would give one of the five- or six-year-olds a pick-a-back ride for a short distance. There was rarely any moment when a small hand was not clutching at Gladys's jacket.

Seven nights out fom Yangcheng found them camped in the heart of a mountainous region unknown to her. They had found a small trail which led southwards. It was not yet dark, but everyone was too exhausted to move farther. The thin, home-made cloth shoes, which everyone wore, were practically all worn out. The big girls' feet were cut and bleeding. Everyone was filthy, covered with dust and dirt; they had no food. Gladys raised her head to scan the party lying in huddled groups under the rocks. She did not like what she saw; unless they received food and help very soon, she was afraid of what might happen to them. Suddenly she saw Teh and Liang ,who were still acting as forward scouts, running back towards her. They were shouting something which she could not hear, but their obvious excitement presaged danger.

'Men!' they shouted. 'Soldiers!'

Gladys froze in a moment of panic. She put her whistle into her mouth to blow the prearranged signal for the children to scatter, but she did not blow it. If they scattered into this wild terrain they might all be lost and would starve or die in the wilderness. And then, as the boys stumbled towards her, she saw a man in uniform rounding a buttress of rock down the valley, and with a gasping sigh of relief realized that they were Nationalist troops. The children had sighted them also. Their tiredness fell away and they bounded over the rocks to greet the newcomers. Gladys, with the girls, advanced more slowly, and as she walked suddenly heard the sound she dreaded more than any other. The noise of aircraft engines! With a thunder of sound that echoed throughout the valley, two Japanese fighters tore through a cleft in the mountains and hurtled across their heads. Although they must have been hundreds of feet up, their sudden appearance, the abrupt bull-roar of their engines sent a shock wave of panic through everyone in the valley.

She threw herself into the shelter of a rock, glimpsing from the corner of her eye that the girls were doing the same. She crouched, rigid, waiting for the rattle of machine-guns. None came. She looked up, as the planes disappeared, catching sight of the stubby wings, the Rising Sun insignia painted on the fuse-lage. But the airmen were obviously intent on something more important than machine-gunning Nationalist troops or refugees in the mountains. Gladys stood up and looked down the valley. The children had been well trained in their drill in the event of attack by aircraft. They were scrambling up from their hiding places. The Nationalist troops, who had also scattered wildly, were mixed up with the children. They rose from the rocks, laughing together.

There were about fifty soldiers, reinforcements from Honan passing up country to join a Nationalist force farther north. Gladys met the young officer in charge, and explained their predicament, but the problem of the hungry children was being solved spontaneously. Soldiers were diving their hands into knapsacks, and bringing out treasures of sweet foods, and all round she could hear only the 'Ahs!' 'Oohs!' and 'Ohs!' of the delighted children.

The soldiers decided to camp in that spot for the night. They invited Gladys and her brood to stay with them and share their food. It was a feast! They had foodstuffs not seen in Shunsi for years. The children sat round the small fires, stuffing themselves to bursting point. Even Gladys, for the first time on the journey, ate her fill. When the troops moved on at dawn the children waved them a sorrowful good-bye.

Each day now took on something of a nightmare complex. Strangely enough, the young children bore up well. They were used to little food; at night, no matter how hard the ground, they slept to a point of complete insensibility; they woke refreshed and ready to play and gambol next morning. They charged up the mountains, lost their bowls and chop-sticks, cried and protested, but they all remained healthy. Sualan, Ninepence, Lan Hsiang and the other girls were in a pitiful state. The sun had cracked their lips and burnt their faces. Their feet were blistered and sore, and they could only hobble a few hundred yards before they had to rest again.

Nevertheless, no one gave up, and they moved slowly onwards through the mountains. On the twelfth day they came out of the mountains and down through the foothills towards the Yellow River. As usual at this time, the small children's voices were a constant background of complaint.

'Ai-weh-deh, my feet hurt!'

'Ai-weh-deh, I'm hungry!'

'Ai-weh-deh, when shall we stop for the night?'

'Ai-weh-deh, will you carry me?'

'Down below,' she said, 'look over there; the village of Yuan Ku; and beyond it, far away, look, the Yellow River! See it shining in the sunshine!'

'But it is so far away, Ai-weh-deh. And we're so hungry!'

'In the village of Yuan Ku they'll give us food, and then we'll arrive at the Yellow River. And when we cross that we'll all be safe. Now let's sing a song as we march down to the town.'

No band of shipwrecked mariners looking from a raft with

salt-bleared eyes at a friendly shore, no thirsty travellers in the desert beholding an oasis, looked more eagerly at that distant shining ribbon of water than Gladys and the older children. The twelve days since they left Yangcheng had been long and weary ones, now at last they were in sight of relief.

They followed the road which led down from the foothills to the town. It had been badly bombed. Rubble littered the streets and most of the houses were roofless. There was an unaccountable silence about the place as they approached. No dogs ran yapping to meet them. No carriers or coolies moved in the streets. The children ran from house to house, their shrill voices echoing in the courtyards. There was no one there. It was deserted. Then Liang and Teh, the faithful scouts still ahead of the party, reported that they had found an old man. Gladys hurried up to him. He was sitting against a tree in the sunshine, a cone-shaped straw hat on his head, a few white hairs straggling from his chin. His thin legs stuck out from the blue cotton trousers. He had been asleep, and was querulous at being woken.

'Old man, this is Yuan Ku, is it not?' she said loudly.

'Yes, this is Yuan Ku.'

'But where are all the people? Why is the city deserted?'

'They've run away. The Japanese are coming, and they've all run away.'

A thin dribble of saliva ran down his chin. He was toothless and his face was shrunken to the bone.

'Why haven't you gone? Why are you still here?'

'I'm too old to run. I'll sleep here in the sun until the Japanese arrive, and if they kill me, who will care? All my sons are gone. All my family are broken like wheatstalks in the wind. I'll wait for the Japanese and spit at them.'

'But where have all the people gone?'

'Across the Yellow River, away from the Japanese.'

'Then we must go there, too. Are there boats?'

'There were boats once. Now I think you are too late.' He cocked a rheumy old eye at the children crowding round him. 'Where are all these children from? Where are they going?'

'We are refugees journeying to Sian,' she said.

His lips curled contemptuously as he looked at her. 'You are a fool, woman, to bother with all these children. The gods intended a woman to care for a handful of children, not an army.'

Gladys had heard such philosophy in China before. It brushed over her head.

'How far is it to the river?'

'Three miles. Follow the road to the ferry, but you will not find a boat there. The Japanese are coming, and they will not leave their boats to be captured. Go back to the mountains, woman. They are the only safe places!'

'We are going to Sian,' she said simply. She blew her whistle and the children lined up around her. It was Cheia's turn to be carried, so she humped him on her back. 'As soon as we get to the river we shall bathe and wash our clothes,' she said. 'And we shall catch a boat and be safe on the other side. Good-bye, old man, and good luck!'

He did not turn his head to watch them go. He let it slump forward on his chest; he was asleep before they had turned the corner.

They trudged down the dusty path to the river edge. There were reeds along the bank, and little bays edged with sand where the children could splash and paddle in the shallows. They ran towards it, shouting and excited. The river was about a mile across, running swift and deep in the centre. But there were no boats, and no sign of any boats!

Sualan said quietly, 'Where are the boats, Ai-weh-deh?'

'They must come across every now and then,' she answered. 'Perhaps we're too late today. We'll spend the night here on the river bank, so we'll be ready to go aboard the boat first thing tomorrow morning.'

They crouched together in a hollow on the bank. A yellow moon rose above the Yellow River, peering down a great fan of silver to look at them. It was very beautiful, but she had no eyes for its beauty. Birds rustled uneasily in the reeds and occasionally a fish would ripple and leap, the splash disturbing the silver surface. It was quiet and peaceful, but she was much afraid. Where were the boats? Why were there no boats? Was the old man right? Had everyone fled across the river to avoid the Japanese? Were they trapped against this broad ribbon of water? She fell eventually into a deep but uneasy slumber, and dreamed that hordes of little yellow men in round steel helmets, carrying a large flag, bright with the scarlet-and-white insignia of a rising sun, were marching closer and closer.

When she awoke next morning the children were already playing in the shallows. The youngest were calling back, shouting: 'Ai-weh-deh, we are hungry. When shall we have something to eat, Ai-weh-deh?'

'Soon,' she called, 'soon!'

She gathered the older boys around her. 'We must look for food. Back in Yuan Ku, they must have left a few oddments. You must go back and search the houses. Look everywhere. We must find a little food.'

The children went on playing in the shallows. The boys trailed off to look for food in the deserted town of Yuan Ku. Gladys sat on the bank and watched the sun climbing up the sky, reflected blindingly in the surface of the wide river. She felt sick. The children had still not got over their amazement at the sight of so large a river; and they explored and poked in the reeds and shallows along the banks. But curiosity would not fill their bellies for long. 'If only a boat would come!' she thought. 'If only a boat would come!'

Three hours later the boys came back triumphant. They had scavenged through most of the houses in Yuan Ku, and each bore some small contribution: a few pounds of mouldy millet in the bottom of a rotting basket; a few dusty-looking, flat, hard cakes of dough from under a shop counter. It was all boiled in the communal pot over a fire of dried reeds, and the result ladled carefully into the forest of waving basins. There was not enough for Gladys or Sualan or the older boys, but the younger children were fed.

The sun rose high, and still no boat moved on the surface of the river. The boys went off to search for more food along the banks; there were a few scattered houses there. She sat quietly watching the children, half alert for the distant rifle fire that would herald the approach of the enemy. The boys came back with a few more scraps of food, which she hoarded for the next day. That night the children huddled together on the bank of the river and whimpered before they went to sleep.

'Ai-weh-deh, we're hungry.'

'Ai-weh-deh, when are we going to cross the river? When are we going to cross the river, Ai-weh-deh?'

She comforted them as best she could, and one by one they dropped off to sleep. The cold, white moon came up from the opposite bank and set in the sky looking at them. A little cold wind rustled in the reeds with a dry, thin rattle. Scarves of opalescent white mist hung above the surface. The water noises were soft, muted. Gladys lay on her back and looked up at the stars. Somehow, it was easier at night. In the sunshine the grim reality of that immense water barrier, the lack of food, the whimpering children, was a burden so heavy as to be almost insupportable. But at night the edges of the present and future were blurred; softened and eased by the slow falling through the peace which preceded sleep. There were a few short hours of forgetfulness before the hot ball of the sun lifted above the horizon and the yelling swarm of children raced for the water to splash and shout and greet the dawn. And, besides, tomorrow it might all be different. Tomorrow a boat might come.

They ate the last crumbs of food on the third day at the bank of the Yellow River. The sun rose and the children grew tired of racing along the banks. She told them stories and her eyes were sore from staring at the water in search of a boat. As the sun went down again, they crept close to her so that she could touch them with her hands. On the morning of the fourth day even the youngest children had caught the mood of despair. It was then that Sualan said:

'Ah-weh-deh, do you remember telling us how Moses took the children of Israel to the waters of the Red Sea. And how God commanded the water to open and the Israelites crossed in safety?'

'Yes, I remember,' she said quietly.

'Then why does not God open the waters of the Yellow River for us to cross?'

She looked wearily at the pretty, childish face, the ingenuous wide eyes. 'I am not Moses, Sualan,' she said.

'But God is always God, Ai-weh-deh. You have told us so a hundred times. If He is God He can open the river for us.'

For a moment she did not know what to say. How to tell a hungry child on the banks of an immense and wide-flowing river that miracles were not just for the asking. How to say, perhaps we are not worthy of a miracle. How to say, although I can face a mortal enemy wherever he may beset me, I cannot open these vast waters. I have no power other than the power of my own faith.

She said: 'Let you and I kneel down and pray, Sualan. And perhaps soon our prayers will be answered.'

The Chinese Nationalist officer commanding the platoon scouting on the wrong side of the river looked back at the section of men straggling along behind him. They were boys, all of them, boys pressed from hinterland villages with rifles shoved into their hands, and ill-fitting uniforms on to their backs, quickly acquiring the ability to live off the land as an elementary part of their military and self-survival training. There were eight of them: unshaven, their heads closely cropped.

Oh, they would fight. If they ran into a probing Japanese patrol they would go to ground, and the bullets from their rifles would kick up tiny geysers of dust around the feet of the enemy. They would hold them for a while, unless the other patrol had a mortar. Or unless they whistled up one of their fighter planes to spray them out of existence with cannon-shells. They would hang on as best they could until nightfall, if possible. Nightfall would save them. Then they could signal their comrades on the far bank, and the precious boat camouflaged with reeds could be pushed out into the river and ferried across. Enough face would be saved by nightfall.

The young officer flicked a fly from his sweaty forehead and sucked in his breath.

His wandering thoughts suddenly jarred to a standstill. A noise! An odd noise! A far off, high pitched sound, wavering and uncertain. A plane? His men thought so; he watched them thumb back their helmets and roll their eyes round the cloudless sky in an effort to locate it. There had been an unusual lack of air activity up and down the Yellow River for the past week. Usually the Jap planes patrolled and fired at anything that moved, even firing bursts into the reed beds at the sides of the river, and occasionally loosing off a sustained burst into the river itself so that a momentary barrier of furious water heaved up in a wall of hissing intimidation.

And yet this sounded almost like singing. Faint and far away, high and monotonous, the sexless piping of many children? He shook his head as though to clear it. The river at this point was a mile wide; there might be children left in the village on the other side of the river. Perhaps they were teaching school; but would their voices carry this far? He mounted a slight rise in the bank, crawling carefully to the top. He raised himself to see better, and grunted in astonishment. He reached for his binoculars and focused. It was an astonishing sight. A great crowd of children were assembled on the bank, all seated in a circle and singing loudly. Some smaller ones were splashing and jumping in the shallows.

He motioned his men back with a hand signal. 'Wait here,' he said. 'It may be a trick. Be alert.'

The Japanese had driven refugees before them on many other occasions. And who were these children? All refugees had left this area days ago. The river was officially closed. As he walked along the bank, he could see that they were Chinese children all right. They saw him, the young ones, and raced towards him, gurgling and shouting with delight.

'Ai-weh-deh,' they screamed, 'here's a soldier. A soldier.'

The young officer noticed the small woman sitting on the ground. She was thin, hungry looking. She got to her feet as he approached, and with a shock of surprise he realized that she was a foreigner.

'Are you mad?' he said. 'Who are you.'

'We are refugees trying to reach Sian,' she said simply.

Her Chinese was excellent, though she spoke with the heavy dialect of the north, but although she was small like his own countrywomen, and her hair dark, he knew she was a foreigner.

'This will soon be a battlefield. Don't you realize that?' he said.

'All China is a battlefield,' she said drearily.

'Are you in charge of these children?'

'Yes, I am in charge of them. We are trying to cross the river.'

He looked at her directly. She was quite a young woman. Her dark hair was scraped back into a bun, her clothes old and soiled; there were dark circles under her eyes, and her face had a sallow, unhealthy look.

'You are a foreigner?'

'Yes, I am a foreigner.'

'For a foreigner you chose a strange occupation.'

She looked steadily at him as he said, 'I think I can get you a boat. It will need three journeys to take you all across, and it is dangerous. If a Japanese plane comes over when you are half-way there will be little hope.'

'We *must* cross the river.'

'You will probably manage to get food in the village on the other side. The people do not like to leave their homes even when the Japanese come.'

'I understand,' she said. 'It was like that with us in Yang-cheng.'

He walked to the river edge, inserted his fingers in his mouth and whistled loudly three times in a peculiar fashion. From across the river came three answering whistles. Two little figures far away on the other bank pushed a boat into the water and began to scull it across.

'I cannot thank you enough,' she said. 'I thought it was the end of us when we couldn't cross the river.'

The young officer noticed her sway a little as one of the children pushed against her.

He looked at her curiously. 'You are ill,' he said. 'You should find a doctor. The Nationalist troops on the other side of the river will have a doctor.'

'I am all right,' she said. 'When we get to Sian I shall be all right.'

With shouts of glee the children filled the boat. The soldiers ferried them rapidly to the other side. They returned and more of the children piled in. On the third journey the soldier helped the foreign woman into the boat with the last group of children. His platoon had gathered round to help. As the boat moved away from the bank, he called his men to attention and gravely saluted. He called: 'Good luck, foreigner!'

He turned to walk back along the bank to his platoon. As he walked he looked into the sky, and listened for the drone of Japanese planes. None came. It was curious about that foreigner. If this had been close to a large city or a settlement, he could have understood it, but wandering across a battlefield escorting an army of ragged Chinese children; that was, indeed, very curious.

They found a village two or three miles back from the bank of the Yellow River and the people were hospitable to them. Although many hundreds of refugees had passed through, they still found food to spare for the children. The Village Elder apportioned so many to each house down the main street, and when their initial hunger was appeased the children scampered from house to house to see how the others were faring. Gladys heard their shrill questions 'What are you eating in your house?' 'We've got *bingsies*. What have you got?' 'We've got *mientiao*!' 'Oh, rotten old mientiao. You can keep it!' 'But we've got rice cakes as well, see!'

It was just as well, thought Gladys wearily – just as well they didn't bother where the next meal was coming from.

They stayed in the village only long enough to finish the food, and then moved on. If the Japanese were approaching the river she wished to get as far away from it as possible. They spent that night in the fields, and went on again next morning to the town of Mien Chih. It, too, was badly bombed, but an old woman directed her to a refugee organization. She found it situated in the old temple; there were cauldrons of steaming food; they were made welcome. And then the police arrived. The inspector was a fat and fussy little man bulging with a sense of his own dignity. He marched up to Gladys, and there was a touch of Alice in Wonderland about his conversation.

'I understand,' he said, 'that you say you have just crossed the Yellow River.'

'Yes!'

'Then you are under arrest. You could not have crossed the Yellow River.'

'Under arrest. But what for?'

'You say you crossed the Yellow River.'

'Yes.'

'No one else crossed with you?'

'No . . . only the children.'

'If nobody else could get across, how did you get across?'

She shook her head in bewilderment. 'We met a soldier who signalled a boat.'

'You could not have met a soldier who signalled a boat. You could not have crossed the river. You are under arrest!' He pursed his lips seriously. This was obviously the most interesting crime he had had committed in his area for some time.

'You didn't expect me to stay there and wait for the Japanese, did you?' she said heatedly. 'And if you arrest me, you'll have to arrest all the children too.'

A little pucker of astonishment creased the blandly official face at this new complication.

'You mean to tell me you are in charge of all these children?'

'I am, and there's no one else to look after them.' She was tired; it was late; and she wanted to rest. She tried wheedling.

'Why don't you leave us alone tonight? I'll come down to your yamen, or the police station, or whatever it is first thing tomorrow morning, and you can arrest me then.'

The fat little policeman looked a little dubious. 'I shall have to examine you before the Mandarin,' he said importantly.

'Well, I shan't try and escape with all these children, shall I? I'll come down to the yamen tomorrow morning and you can ask all the questions you want.'

He had to be satisfied with that. He went off into the growing darkness, and Gladys wearily spread out her bedding; it appeared that escaping officialdom was almost as difficult as escaping from the Japanese.

Next morning, with the children, at the head of her party, Gladys marched down to the yamen to be interrogated. The children were not allowed inside, and rumours that something awful was going to happen to Ai-weh-deh had spread among them. They stood in a block outside the front door, and as soon as she went inside kept up an increasing chant 'Let her out! Let her out! Let her out!'

The Mandarin was a benign-looking elder who showed that he had little sympathy with the policeman, whose evidence was both repetitive and absurd.

'You say you crossed the Yellow River?'

'Yes.'

'I say you did not!'

'But I tell you we did,' Gladys protested. 'How could I have got from Shansi to Honan unless I crossed the river?'

'Then how could you have crossed without a boat?'

'We crossed in a boat! A soldier signalled a boat!'

'Then you have committed a crime. You will please examine this document.' From the hands of one of his orderlies he produced a massive and important-looking scroll, and handed it across.

Gladys scanned it. Among the seals and important looking hieroglyphics, she read that by decree of the General Commanding the Nationalist armies in that region, the Yellow River was closed to all traffic. No one could cross, or journey upon it. The order was dated five days previously.

'So that's why there were no boats,' said Gladys. 'I wondered why.'

'Do you admit now that you have committed this crime?' thundered the little policeman.

'Of course I have,' retorted Gladys angrily. 'We are refugees from Shansi proceeding to Sian. There are a hundred children with me. You didn't expect us to wait on the other side to be killed, did you?'

Outside, the chant of the children went on monotonously. 'Let her out! Let her out!' And now they had found the windows, and a dozen small faces were peering through, and tapping the panes with their fingers.

'Let her out! Let her out!'

The Mandarin had had enough. 'It is plain,' he said, 'that if this woman has committed an offence it is of the smallest technical nature.' He smiled at her. 'If you can control your children for a few minutes, I think I might be able to help you.'

She went outside. A few sharp words and a few indiscriminate cuffs got the children into order. She went back to see the Mandarin. The policeman had disappeared.

'Every morning,' he said, 'a train leaves Mien Chih and travels along the river in the direction of Sian. It does not reach there because something has gone wrong with the line, but at least it will take you some distance on your journey.'

'But we've no tickets and no money for tickets,' said Gladys.

He looked at her gravely. 'In Honan today,' he said, 'all trains are refugee trains. No one is expected to have tickets. Tomorow morning go to the station with your children and get on the train.'

Gladys thanked him, and took the children back to the refugee centre. That afternoon she led them all to a pond on the edge of the city, and they tried to wash off the worst of the dirt from their clothes and bodies. In the evening she assembled them in the courtyard and addressed them.

'You all know what a train is, don't you?' she said.

There was an excited babble of conversation. No, most of them didn't know what a train was. What was it? They'd never heard of such a thing.

Gladys demonstrated with sound effects, and 'Oohs!' and 'Ahs!' of delighted anticipation greeted her description. Sualan, Ninepence, Teh, Liang, the older boys and girls were, on the surface, more sophisticated about the approaching experience. Of course, they had heard about trains. What was there to get excited about? But they were excited, nevertheless.

'Tomorrow you will line up with clean hands and faces, and anyone with a dirty face or dirty hands will not be allowed on that train.' Her speech over, the children scattered, to play about and terrorize the other refugees in the temple, before clambering into their bedding, chattering eagerly of the wondrous experience that was to befall them next day. They dropped off quickly into the sound sleep of the very young, and very innocent, within minutes of feeling their quilts around them.

They were all up at dawn next morning, eagerly tying up their bundles, scrambling to be first at the great stone basin full of water in the temple courtyard, so that faces and hands should be the requisite colour required by the omnipotent Ai-weh-deh. They lined up to have their basins filled with steaming millet, scooped the thick mixture into open mouths with dexterous chopsticks, and with astounding cooperation formed a long crocodile, before Gladys had even tied up her own bedding.

She thanked the women running the refugee centre, blew her whistle, and with a great laugh and cheer, and an explosion of chatter, they set off for the train. The station was a long raised piece of concrete three feet above the track. Any roof it possessed had been blasted away, long before, by falling bombs. A hundred yards from the platform the railway lines curved out of sight between a jumble of houses. It was upon this bend – on being told that from this direction the train would appear – that a hundred pairs of eyes were focused.

Gladys had lined them up in three straggling ranks. The air was tense with anticipation, and after a few minutes, far off, there came the noise of the train! One hundred children tensed, a little uneasy. Those were very strange noises. Such a whistling anger, such a terrifying rumble and hiss! Eyes twitched towards her and back to that fatal curve. Was Ai-weh-deh quite certain she was right about this 'train' thing? Even in the distance it sounded like the grandfather of all the dragons in the world. Supposing it gobbled them all up? The noise grew greater. Couplings clanked as buffers met; brakes screamed in steel anguish, and round the corner, steaming and blowing and snorting, came the hideous iron terror? There was one loud anguished squeal of utter terror from the children. The ranks dissolved: panic was contagious. Bundles, basins, chopsticks flew into the air. Children fled in every direction. By the time the train was still twenty-five yards away, not a single child remained on the platform. The wooden carriages clattered to a halt. The engine subsided into heavy, steamy breathing, and Gladys tried to collect her charges.

The older boys and girls, already ashamed of their sudden panic, were rounding up the younger ones, plaintively protesting that they had only run away to catch the others. One batch of eight-year-olds were found to have raced all the way back to the refugee centre. Children were retrieved from under boxes and bales from every conceivable hiding-place within 200 yards of the station. Group by group, she assembled them once more on the platform. Fortunately, the train seemed to be in no hurry to go anywhere at all. The carriages were simply wooden boxes with roofs on. There were no seats. And there were many other refugee passengers with their bundles and basins.

She managed to pile all the children into one long carriage and when, an hour later, the train jogged slowly into motion, the children began to enjoy their experience. There was only one other moment of panic. About two hours later an elderly Chinese gentleman sitting a few yards from Gladys, and surrounded by children, carefully produced a stub of candle from his pocket. He placed it on the floor and tenderly lit it. At least three little boys immediately blew it out. At that moment the train plunged into a tunnel. The darkness was impenetrable; the wails and panic beyond description. The elderly gentleman, after a minute or two, succeeded in relighting the candle, and – the objective of his performance established – no little boy emitted even a zephyr breath in its direction this time.

For four days they stayed aboard the train as it rattled forward in slow, short stages. Occasionally it stopped for hours, and everyone got off and stretched their legs. At intervals along the line there were refugee feeding camps where they were given food and tea. Gladys dozed a great deal of the time. It wasn't that she felt ill; it was as if a general tiredness had settled into her bones. They had been almost three weeks on the road now, soaked by the rains and chilled by the winds. She had slept badly and gone without food for days on end; it was only to be expected, she told herself, that she didn't feel as well as normally.

At the small village of Tiensan the train stopped. It went no farther. An important bridge had been blown up, the lines destroyed. Here the undulating plain ended, and the mountains rose steeply ahead of them. They had to cross those mountains; the train lines continued on the other side. A thin stream of refugees moved up through the rocky passes; old men, young women, fathers, mothers, families laden with bundles, all fleeing westwards away from the malison of the Japanese. They begged for food in the village, and Gladys looked at the high peaks ahead. They frightened her. She didn't want to go on; she just wanted to stop where she was and rest. But she knew it was impossible. Their only hope was Madame Chiang Kai-shek's organization in Sian. Even though the city was still many days' journey away, somehow she had to summon up sufficient reserves of strength to get there. But those mountains! They looked so high and cruel. The sun sank behind them, and every valley and peak was suffused with its crimson glow. At any other time she would have admired the scene: now she thought the world was bathed in blood. Next day they started on their journey.

At first the trail ran upwards. They were all practically bare-footed and the sharp flints cut their feet. Looking back from the first ridges, they could see the dust rising slowly from the plain below; with the red ball of the sun glaring like a demon eye through the haze. For four hours they toiled upwards, the youngsters scrambling ahead, Gladys and the older girls coming up more slowly. From a high shoulder of the mountains they had their last glimpse of the plain; then, as they dropped down following the winding path, the peaks closed them in.

Late in the afternoon Liang and Teh, the inevitable scouts, came back to report a village ahead hidden in a turn of the valley. When Gladys reached it the children were already drinking basins of *mentang*, the water left after the millet had been cooked, and the villagers were sharing amongst them rice cakes and other odd fragments of food. She drank some tea and felt better. The people were kindly. It would take them two more days to cross the mountains and reach Tung Kwan, they told her. There were other villages on the track where they might get food. Slowly she struggled to her feet. Another high ridge stood up against the skyline in front of them. She reckoned that if they could cross that, they could spend the night in the valley beyond. Another hour's climbing and the five-year-olds were already hanging round her coat tails as usual. Four of the fourteen-year-old boys took it in turns to carry them. Gladys carried one also, the big girls being much too tired and weak to help. It was all they could do to stagger along.

The progress of the entire party was very slow now. The sun was sinking before they reached the ridge, and Gladys realized that they would not cross it before dark. The only thing was to find some sheltered spot and spend the night. As upon the previous night, the sun went down in the same stupefying welter of crimson, and darkness came swiftly up out of the valleys to wrap them in. In the overhang of a cliff they found a little shelter and huddled together, seeking warmth. The younger ones were so tired that they were asleep as soon as they were wrapped in their quilted bedding. It quickly got cold, and she could feel the chill striking through to her bones. She wedged herself between two rocks and fell into a deep, troubled sleep.

As soon as it was light, they wrapped up their bedding and set off again, the youngsters tearing off ahead. They crossed the ridge as the sun came up. All round were bare peaks running away in all directions, intimidating and desolate. A chill little thought settled in her mind. If ever they lost the track, they could wander until they died amid such desolation. All that day they filed painfully onwards. It was in the afternoon, seated on a rock for one of their frequent rests, that the break suddenly came.

Her face streaked with lines where the sweat had coursed down the white mountain dust, she stared round at the children. The eight- and nine-year-olds were still ahead, but two dozen of the little ones with mournful faces, the fives and sixes and sevens, were gathered round her, almost too dumb to plead to be carried or be given food or drink. The girls were slumped on the rocks in attitudes of utter dejection. Even Liang and Teh sat glumly, their chins in their hands, worn out by carrying the small ones for hour after hour.

It was then that Gladys felt something wet flowing down her cheek. She tried to flick the tears away, but they only came faster, faster and faster, and soon she was sobbing aloud, abandoning herself to grief, sobbing because she had no strength to stay her tears, sobbing from sheer weakness and exhaustion, sobbing for all the children, for all China, and all the world, so deep was her misery. At that moment she had no heart to go on any farther. She was convinced that they were all finished; that they would all die in the mountains. She was convinced that she had brought them all to this plight, that she had betrayed them, and she sobbed because of her guilt. The children sobbed with her, and the little boys coming back down the trail stood open-mouthed and then, also influenced by the contagion of grief, they too began to wail. For many minutes the sound of their distress echoed in the valley. When it was over Gladys wiped her face with her coat sleeve, and sniffed. The tears had cleansed her soul, washed away the bleak desperation, washed away even a little of the aching tiredness which weakened her will and her determination. She smiled wanly at Sualan, who crouched against her.

'A good cry is always good for you!' she said stoutly. 'Now that's enough, all of you! We'll sing a hymn, and while we're singing it, we shall march down the track to that big buttress of rock. So stand up, everybody, and no more crying. Let's see who can sing the loudest, shall we? One ... two ... three ...'

The mountains in their long years of sun and wind and rain must have seen many strange sights, but it is doubtful if they had seen anything more unusual, or more gallant, than this column of children led by a small woman with a tear-stained face, carolling with such shrill determination as she led her band onward towards the promised land.

– from *The Small Woman*

RICHARD E. BYRD

# Alone in the Antarctic

In 1934 Admiral Richard E. Byrd, the American explorer, was leader
of an expedition in the Antarctic. Its base on the barrier ice of
the Ross Sea was called Little America. 120 miles further south they
had an advance base for weather observation – a wooden shack
which was buried in ice and snow. Admiral Byrd decided to spend
the winter there alone. For five months, he would be inaccessible:
the expedition's tractors could not cross the snow fields in the
dark and extreme cold of the winter night. He was left there at
the end of March, and for two months he enjoyed the solitude. But
at the end of May there was a disaster nobody had foreseen.


Out of the deepening darkness came the cold. On May 19th,
when I took the usual walk, the temperature was 65° below zero.
For the first time the canvas boots failed to protect my feet. One
heel was nipped, and I was forced to return to the hut and
change to reindeer mukluks. That day I felt miserable; my body
was racked by shooting pains – exactly as if I had been gassed.
Very likely I was; in inspecting the ventilator pipes next morning I discovered that the intake pipe was completely clogged
with rime and that the outlet pipe was two-thirds full. Next
day – Sunday the 20th – was the coldest yet. The minimum
thermometer dropped to 72° below zero; the inside thermograph, which always read a bit lower than the instruments in
the shelter, stood at – 74°; and the thermograph in the shelter
was stopped dead – the ink, though well laced with glycerine,
and the lubricant were both frozen. So violently did the air in
the fuel tank expand after the stove was lit that oil went shooting all over the place; to insulate the tank against similar temperature spreads I wrapped around it the rubber air cushion which
by some lucky error had been included among my gear. In the
glow of a flashlight the vapour rising from the stovepipe and
the outlet ventilator looked like the discharge from two
steam engines. My fingers agonized over the thermograph, and

I was hours putting it to rights. The fuel wouldn't flow from the drums; I had to take one inside and heat it near the stove. All day long I kept two primus stoves burning in the tunnel.

Sunday the 20th also brought a radio schedule; I had the devil's own time trying to meet it. The engine balked for an hour; my fingers were so brittle and frostbitten from tinkering with the carburettor that, when I actually made contact with Little America, I could scarcely work the key. 'Ask Haines come on,' was my first request. While Hutcheson searched the tunnels of Little America for the Senior Meteorologist, I chatted briefly with Charlie Murphy. Little America claimed only – 60°. 'But we're moving the brass monkeys below,' Charlie advised. 'Seventy-one below here now,' I said. 'You can have it,' was the closing comment from the north.

Then Bill Haines's merry voice sounded in the ear-phones. I explained the difficulty with the thermograph. 'Same trouble we've had,' Bill said. 'It's probably due to frozen oil. I'd suggest you bring the instrument inside, and try soaking it in gasolene, to cut whatever oil traces remain. Then rinse it in ether. As for the ink's freezing, you might try adding more glycerine.' Bill was in a jovial mood. 'Look at me, Admiral,' he boomed. 'I never have any trouble with the instruments. The trick is in having an ambitious and docile assistant.' I really chuckled over that because I knew, from the first expedition, what Grimminger, the Junior Meteorologist, was going through; Bill, with his back to the fire and blandishment on his tongue, persuading the recruit that duty and the opportunity for self-improvement required him to go up into the blizzard to fix a balky trace; Bill humming to himself in the warmth of a shack while the assistant in an open pit kept a theodolite trained on the sounding balloon soaring into the night, and stuttered into a telephone the different vernier readings from which Bill was calculating the velocities and directions of the upper air currents. That day I rather wished that I, too, had an assistant. He would have taken his turn on the anemometer pole, no mistake. The frost in the iron cleats went through the fur soles of the mukluks, and froze the balls of my feet. My breath made little explosive sounds on the wind; my lungs, already sore, seemed to shrivel when I breathed.

Seldom had the aurora flamed more brilliantly. For hours the night danced to its frenetic excitement. And at times the sound of Barrier quakes was like that of heavy guns. My tongue was swollen and sore from drinking scalding hot tea, and the tip of my nose ached from frost-bite. A big wind, I guessed, would come out of this still cold; it behoved me to look at my roof. I carried gallons of water topside, and poured it around the edges of the shack. It froze almost as soon as it hit. The ice was an armour plating over the packed drift.

At midnight, when I clambered topside for an auroral 'ob', a wild sense of suffocation came over me the instant I pushed my shoulders through the trapdoor. My lungs gasped, but no air reached them. Bewildered and perhaps a little frightened, I slid down the ladder and lunged into the shack. In the warm air the feeling passed as quickly as it had come. Curious but cautious, I again made my way up the ladder. And again the same thing happened; I lost my breath, but I perceived why. A light air was moving down from eastward; and its bitter touch, when I faced into it, was constricting the breathing passages. So I turned my face away from it, breathing into my glove; and in that attitude finished the 'ob'. Before going below, I made an interesting experiment. I put a thermometer on the snow, let it lie there awhile, and discovered that the temperature at the surface was actually 5° colder than at the level of the instrument shelter, four feet higher. Reading in the sleeping bag afterwards, I froze one finger, although I shifted the book steadily from one hand to the other, slipping the unoccupied hand into the warmth of the bag.

Out of the cold and out of the east came the wind. It came on gradually, as if the sheer weight of the cold were almost too much to be moved. On the night of the 21st the barometer started down. The night was black as a thunderhead when I made my first trip topside; and a tension in the wind, a bulking of shadows in the night indicated that a new storm centre was forming. Next morning, glad of an excuse to stay underground,

I worked a long time on the Escape Tunnel by the light of a
red candle standing in a snow recess. That day I pushed the
emergency exit to a distance of twenty-two feet, the farthest
it was ever to go. My stint done, I sat down on a box, thinking
how beautiful was the red of the candle, how white the rough-
hewn snow. Soon I became aware of an increasing clatter of the
anemometer cups. Realizing that the wind was picking up, I
went topside to make sure that everything was secured. It is a
queer experience to watch a blizzard rise. First there is the wind,
rising out of nowhere. Then the Barrier unwrenches itself from
quietude; and the surface, which just before had seemed as hard
and polished as metal, begins to run like a making sea. Sometimes, if the wind strikes hard, the drift comes across the Barrier
like a hurrying white cloud, tossed hundreds of feet into the
air. Other times the growth is gradual. You become conscious
of a general slithering movement on all sides. The air fills with
tiny scraping and sliding and rustling sounds as the first loose
crystals stir. In a little while they are moving as solidly as an
incoming tide, which creams over the ankles, then surges to the
waist, and finally is at the throat. I have walked in drift so
thick as not to be able to see a foot ahead of me; yet, when I
glanced up, I could see the stars shining through the thin layer
just overhead.

Smoking tendrils were creeping up the anemometer pole
when I finished my inspection. I hurriedly made the trapdoor
fast, as a sailor might batten down a hatch; and knowing that
my ship was well secured, I retired to the cabin to ride out the
storm. It could not reach me, hidden deep in the Barrier crust;
nevertheless the sounds came down. The gale sobbed in the
ventilators, shook the stovepipe until I thought it would be
jerked out by the roots, pounded the roof with sledge-hammer
blows. I could actually feel the suction effect through the per-
vious snow. A breeze flickered in the room and the tunnels. The
candles wavered and went out. My only light was the feeble
storm lantern.

Even so, I didn't have any idea how really bad it was until
I went aloft for an observation. As I pushed back the trap-door,
the drift met me like a moving wall. It was only a few steps from

the ladder to the instrument shelter, but it seemed more like a mile. The air came at me in snowy rushes; I breasted it as I might a heavy surf. No night had ever seemed so dark. The beam from the flashlight was choked in its throat; I could not see my hand before my face.

My windproofs were caked with drift by the time I got below. I had a vague feeling that something had changed while I was gone, but what, I couldn't tell. Presently I noticed that the shack was appreciably colder. Raising the stove lid, I was surprised to find that the fire was out, though the tank was half full. I decided that I must have turned off the valve unconsciously before going aloft; but, when I put a match to the burner, the draught down the pipe blew out the flame. The wind, then, must have killed the fire. I got it going again, and watched it carefully.

The blizzard vaulted to gale force. Above the roar the deep, taut thrumming note of the radio antenna and the anemometer guy wires reminded me of wind in a ship's rigging. The wind direction trace turned scratchy on the sheet; no doubt drift had short-circuited the electric contacts, I decided. Realizing that it was hopeless to attempt to try to keep them clear, I let the instrument be. There were other ways of getting the wind direction. I tied a handkerchief to a bamboo pole and ran it through the outlet ventilator; with a flashlight I could tell which way the cloth was whipped. I did this at hourly intervals, noting any change of direction on the sheet. But by 2 o'clock in the morning I had had enough of this periscope sighting. If I expected to sleep and at the same time maintain the continuity of the records, I had no choice but to clean the contact points.

The wind was blowing hard then. The Barrier shook from the concussions overhead; and the noise was as if the entire physical world were tearing itself to pieces. I could scarcely heave the trapdoor open. The instant it came clear I was plunged into a blinding smother. I came out crawling, clinging to the handle of the door until I made sure of my bearings. Then I let the door fall shut, not wanting the tunnel filled with drift. To see was impossible. Millions of tiny pellets exploded in my eyes, stinging like BB shot. It was even hard to breathe, because snow instantly clogged the mouth and nostrils. I made my way towards the anemometer pole on hands and knees, scared that I might be bowled off my feet if I stood erect; one false step and I should be lost for ever.

I found the pole all right; but not until my head collided with a cleat. I managed to climb it, too, though ten million ghosts were tearing at me, ramming their thumbs into my eyes. But the errand was useless. Drift as thick as this would mess up the contact points as quickly as they were cleared; besides, the wind cups were spinning so fast that I stood a good chance of losing a couple of fingers in the process. Coming down the pole, I had a sense of being whirled violently through the air, with no control over my movements. The trapdoor was completely buried when I found it again, after scraping around for some time with my mittens. I pulled at the handle, first with one hand, then with both. It did not give. It's a tight fit, anyway, I mumbled to myself. The drift has probably wedged the corners. Standing astride the hatch, I braced myself and heaved with all my strength. I might just as well have tried hoisting the Barrier.

Panic took me then, I must confess. Reason fled. I clawed at the three-foot square of timber like a madman. I beat on it with my fists, trying to shake the snow loose; and, when that did no good, I lay flat on my belly and pulled until my hands went weak from cold and weariness. Then I crooked my elbow, put my face down, and said over and over again, You damn fool, you damn fool. Here for weeks I had been defending myself against the danger of being penned inside the shack; instead, I was now locked out; and nothing could be worse, especially since I had only a wool parka and pants under my wind-proofs. Just two feet below was sanctuary – warmth, food, tools, all the means of survival. All these things were an arm's length away, but I was powerless to reach them.

There is something extravagantly insensate about an Antarctic blizzard at night. Its vindictiveness cannot be measured on an anemometer sheet. It is more than just wind; it is a solid wall of snow moving at gale force, pounding like surf.* The whole malevolent rush is concentrated upon you as upon a personal enemy. In the senseless explosion of sound you are reduced to a crawling thing on the margin of a disintegrating world; you can't see, you can't hear, you can hardly move. The lungs gasp after the air is sucked out of them, and the brain is shaken. Nothing in the world will so quickly isolate a man.

Half-frozen, I stabbed towards one of the ventilators, a few feet away. My mittens touched something round and cold. Cupping it in my hands, I pulled myself up. This was the outlet ventilator. Just why, I don't know – but instinct made me kneel and press my face against the opening. Nothing in the room was visible, but a dim patch of light illuminated the floor, and warmth rose up to my face. That steadied me.

Still kneeling, I turned my back to the blizzard and considered what might be done. I thought of breaking in the windows in the roof, but they lay two feet down in hard crust, and were reinforced with wire besides. If I only had something to dig with, I could break the crust and stamp the windows in with my feet. The pipe cupped between my hands supplied the first inspiration; maybe I could use that to dig with. It, too, was wedged tight; I pulled until my arms ached, without budging it; I had lost all track of time, and the despairing thought came to me that I was lost in a task without an end. Then I remembered the shovel. A week before, after levelling drift from the last light blow, I had stabbed a shovel handle up in the crust somewhere to leeward. That shovel would save me. But how to find it in the avalanche of the blizzard?

I lay down and stretched out full length. Still holding the pipe, I thrashed around with my feet, but pummelled only empty air. Then I worked back to the hatch. The hard edges at the opening provided another grip, and again I stretched out and kicked. Again no luck. I dared not let go until I had something else familiar to cling to. My foot came up against the other

---

*Because of this blinding, suffocating drift, in the Antarctic, winds of only moderate velocity have the punishing force of full-fledged hurricanes elsewhere.

ventilating pipe. I edged back to that, and from the new anchorage repeated the manoeuvre. This time my ankle struck something hard. When I felt it and recognized the handle, I wanted to caress it.

Embracing this thrice-blessed tool, I inched back to the trapdoor. The handle of the shovel was just small enough to pass under the little wooden bridge which served as a grip. I got both hands on the shovel and tried to wrench the door up; my strength was not enough, however. So I lay down flat on my belly and worked my shoulders under the shovel. Then I heaved, the door sprang open, and I rolled down the shaft. When I tumbled into the light, and warmth of the room, I kept thinking, how wonderful, how perfectly wonderful.

My wrist watch had stopped; the chronometers showed that I had been gone just under an hour. The stove had blown out again, but I did not bother to light it. Enough warmth remained for me to undress. I was exhausted; it was all I could do to hoist myself into the bunk. But I did not sleep at first. The blizzard scuffled and pounded gigantically overhead; and my mind refused to drop the thought of what I might still be doing if the shovel hadn't been there. Still struggling, probably. Or maybe not. There are harder ways to die than freezing to death. The lush numbness and the peace that lulls the mind when the ears cease listening to the blizzard's ridiculous noise, could make death seem easy.

The wind was still blowing, but not so violently, when I awakened at 7 o'clock the next morning. Dressing in the yellow light of the storm lantern, I shivered in every bone. My clothes, rigid with frost, lay in a grotesque heap on the floor, exactly as they had fallen a few hours before; they crackled like paper when I put them on. Starting up the ladder, I thought glumly. It will be stuck again for sure. Therefore, I had no misgivings at finding the door jammed. Armed with a saw, a shovel, alpine rope, and a lantern, I walked to the far end of the Escape Tunnel. It didn't take long to breach a hole in the roof, which was less than two feet thick at this point.

Before leaving the tunnel, I drove a stout stick into the roof, to which I made fast one end of the line. With the other end secured to my belt, I clambered to the surface over a ladder made of boxes. The drift was still heavy, but with a flashlight it was possible to see a yard or two. After a couple of false stabs I finally fetched the anemometer pole. The drift packed in the cups was almost as compact as cement; I cleaned them out and scraped the contact points. It was an abominable task; but it had to be done, because the fouling slowed down the cups and hence the wind-speed reading. Yet, after what I had been through the night before, there was little reason to complain.

For once, 'daily promenade' was missed. Every moment that could be spared from the instruments and my own personal needs was devoted to levelling drift around the shack. Luckily the new snow wasn't packed hard. I just shovelled it into the air and let the wind dissipate it to leeward. That done, I sealed off the breach of the Escape Tunnel with the sides of a couple of food boxes and reopened the hatch. The faint lightening in the gloom that came with midday was draining away; heavy shadows were pressing down through the ghostly billowing of drift. But the wind was spent; and so was the cold, temporarily. The temperature kited to 10° below. Safe in the bunk, I slept the sleep of a man who had been working a hundred years.

Thursday the 24th was unbelievably warm. At the 8 a.m. 'ob' the maximum thermometer read 2° above zero. The wind still haunted the east; and puffs of drift came erratically from that quarter, thickening the steady fall of snow from the sky. I was nearly an hour late meeting the radio schedule, because the antenna had blown down and I didn't find it out until after I had checked the transmitter and receiver. I made a hurried splice at a break and re-rigged the antenna temporarily on two poles. Dyer was still calling patiently when I made contact. My signals, he said, were weak but intelligible. Beyond discussing arrangements for me to participate in a special broadcast, we had little to talk about. At Little America the temperature was 25° above zero, and Bill Haines officially announced a 'heat wave'.

I was informed that on Saturday Little America was broadcasting a special programme to the Chicago World Fair; would I mind adding my greetings? Certainly not. It was agreed that I should spell out in code, 'Greeting from the bottom of the world,' which message was to be picked up and relayed by Little America's more powerful transmitter. I reduced the message to dots and dashes and practised religiously. When Saturday came, Charlie Murphy broke the news just before the broadcast, that New York now wanted me to spell, 'Antarctic greetings,' instead. 'I'm given to understand,' he said sententiously, 'they intend to translate the damn thing into fireworks.'

'Let it be on their own heads, then,' I said.

Charlie chuckled, 'If the fireworks are supposed to spell out what you send, then Chicago is in for the wildest display since the Fire.'

As excited as an actor making his debut, I sat at Advance Base listening to the broadcast from Little America; and when somebody said, 'We shall now attempt to make contact with Admiral Byrd,' I reached for the key and worked it furiously. But it went for nought. Dyer reported a few minutes after that he had heard it clearly, but Chicago hadn't heard anything. 'No doubt the fireworks went off anyway,' he observed dryly.

Bill Haines's forecast of a 'heat wave' was no jest. That afternoon the thermometer rose to 18° above zero – the second highest point it ever reached. The wind, dallying in the east, flooded the Barrier with warm air from the distant ocean. From then until the end of the month the coldest temperature recorded was 23° below zero; and most of the time it was above zero or close to it. Snow fell in a relentless flutter; the Barrier became a concentrated gloom, except when the moon fetched back on its fortnightly errand, was able to break through the cloud rack and bathe it briefly in an astringent light.*

*Studied as a whole, the records show that May was not exactly a hot month. The cold passed 40° below zero 20 days out of the 31, crossed 50° below, 12 days; crossed 60° below, 3 days; and 70° below 2 days.

*May 25*

This is my sixty-fourth day at Advance Base, and it just so happened that I had some leisure time. I have been taking advantage of this to think back over my stay here and take stock of my situation.

There are three things for which I am particularly thankful. The first is that my records so far are complete (though blotted and splotched a bit). The second is that my defences are perfected, and the third is that I have become well adjusted to conditions – especially psychologically. I feel able now to withstand any assaults the beleaguering night may launch. Indeed, look forward to the rest of my sojourn with pleasure.

Though I am not quite as heavy as when I came out here, I feel all right. I was probably a bit overweight, anyway. Perhaps the fumes have had something to do with the lost pounds, though because of my precautions I think I am getting less fumes than at first.

I am finding that life here has become largely a life of the mind. Unhurried reflection is a sort of companion. Yes, solitude is greater than I anticipated. My sense of values is changing, and many things which before were in solution in my mind now seem to be crystallizing. I am better able to tell what in the world is wheat for me and what is chaff. In fact, my definition of success itself is changing. Just lately my views about man and his place in the cosmic scheme have begun to run something like this:

If I had never seen a watch and should see one for the first time, I should be sure its hands were moving according to some plan and not at random. Nor does it seem any more reasonable for me to conceive that the precision and order of the universe is the product of blind chance. This whole concept is summed up in the word harmony. For those who seek it, there is inexhaustible evidence of an all-pervading intelligence.

The human race, my intuition tells me, is not outside the cosmic process and is not an accident. It is as much a part of the universe as the trees, the mountains, the aurora, and the stars. My reason approves this and the findings of science, as I see them, point in the same direction. And, since man is a part of the cosmos and subject to its laws, I see no reason to doubt that these same natural laws operate in the psychological as well as in the physical sphere and that their operation is manifest in the workings of the consciousness.

Therefore, it seems to me that convictions of right and wrong, being, as they are, products of the consciousness, must also be formed in accordance with these laws. I look upon the conscience as the mechanism which makes us directly aware of them and their significance and serves as a link with the universal intelligence which gives them form and harmoniousness.

I believe further that the age-tested convictions of right and wrong, in which individual aberrations must have been largely cancelled out, are as much a manifestation of cosmic law and intelligence as are all other phenomena.

Therefore, the things that mankind has tested and found right make for harmony and progress – or peace; and the things it has found wrong hinder progress and make for discord. The right things lead to rational behaviour – such as the substitution of reason for force – and so to freedom. The wrong things lead to brute force and slavery.

But the peace I describe is not passive. It must be won. Real peace comes from struggle that involves such things as effort, discipline, enthusiasm. This is also the way to strength. An inactive peace may lead to sensuality and flabbiness, which are discordant. It is often necessary to fight to lessen discord. This is the paradox.

When a man achieves a fair measure of harmony within himself and his family circle, he achieves peace; and a nation made up of such individuals and groups is a happy nation. As the harmony of a star in its course is expressed by rhythm and grace, so the harmony of a man's life-course is expressed by happiness; this, I believe, is the prime desire of mankind.

'The universe is an almost untouched reservoir of significance and value,' and man need not be discouraged because he cannot fathom it. His view of life is no more than a flash in time. The details and distractions are infinite. It is only natural, therefore, that we should never see the picture whole. But the universal goal – the attainment of harmony – is apparent. The very act of perceiving this goal and striving constantly towards it does much in itself to bring us closer and, therefore, becomes an end in itself.

Snow was still falling on Thursday the 31st. The morning was dreary and stagnant; the temperature about 5° above. The calendar warned: 'Radio schedule'. I went about the preparations methodically. Before me now are the messages which I dispatched to Little America that day. One was to Chief Pilot June and Navigator Rawson, reminding them to swing the planes for compass deviations. Another was to my wife, suggesting that she take up with my secretary, Miss McKercher, and my representatives in the United States ways and means of reducing the expedition's expenses.

Dyer took these messages down, then read them back. Poulter, he said, had already arrived in the radio shack in response to my summons. I had a long talk with him and Charlie Murphy over the proposed operations, and was particularly emphatic about the dangers from crevasses confronting the tractors. Poulter finished his business with me; and Charlie Murphy stayed to finish a few matters, one having to do with the engagement of an ice pilot for the *Jacob Ruppert* on her voyage to Little America in December. We talked back and forth nearly an hour and a half. From my desk in the shack I could hear the engine in the tunnel; for some reason it started skipping. 'Wait,' I spelled out to Dyer. Unhooking the lantern, I went into the tunnel. The air was thick with exhaust gases. Thinking the mixture was at fault, I bent over the carburettor and tinkered with the needle valve. This had little effect. I remember straightening up. And that was the last conscious act of mine that I do remember. The next thing I recall, I was down on my hands and knees; and through the drowsiness, like an echo from far away, came an insistent notion that something terribly important ought to be done. What it was exactly my mind couldn't tell; and I felt helpless to do anything about it. I don't know how long I remained in that position. It may be that the cold aroused me. Anyhow, after a little while I crawled into the shack. The radio desk emerged from the blur, and then I remembered what I was supposed to do. I fumbled for the key

and signed off, thinking how hard it was to spell out what I had
to say. If any acknowledgement came, I did not hear it; for
I couldn't get the earphones on.*

My actions thereafter are uncertain; I don't really know
which were nightmare and which were fact. I remember lying
on the bunk, fully dressed, and hearing, as if with surprise, the
irregular beat of the engine in the tunnel and realizing that I
must shut it off to escape asphyxiation. I rolled off the bunk
and staggered to the door. Dizziness seized me, and my heart
turned fantastic somersaults; but, as from a great distance, I
could see the grey fumes of the exhaust smoke curling under
the top sill; and the upper half of the tunnel, when I entered,
was so foggy that I could not see as far as the alcove where the
engine lay.

Very probably I dropped to my hands and knees, as I must
have appreciated the necessity for keeping my head under the
fumes and in the uncontaminated air near the floor. Anyhow,
I was on my knees when I reached into the recess and threw
the ignition switch. When I turned around, the light was
gone in the doorway; this was puzzling until I recalled that
the only light in the shack was the electric bulb over the radio
desk, which burned only while the engine supplied current.
Luckily the lantern was still burning on a box, where I had
set it down before adjusting the engine. Pushing the lantern
ahead of me, I crawled back to the shack and to the bunk.

Whatever did, in fact, occur during the rest of this last day
in May, this I do know; that much of it was probably fantasy
– a slow and wearying fantasy. Perhaps I did in truth roll off
the bunk and try to replace the sheets on the register drum;
else how to account for the vague recollection of seeing the
glass frame on the floor some time in the afternoon. But the
rest of it – the skyrocketing pain in my forehead and eyes,
the nausea, the violent beating of my heart, the illusion of
being a thin flame drawn between two voids – they could not

*The radio log at Little America shows that twenty minutes or so
elapsed between the time I said, 'Wait' and the time I signed off,
saying, 'See you Sunday.' This fixes approximately the interval I
was in the tunnel.

have been real. Only the cold was real: the numbness in the hands and feet, creeping like a slow paralysis through my body. At least, I could cope with cold. I grasped for the throat of the sleeping bag, and eased in.

Once the ticking of the clocks roused me out of the stupor. I have no sure memory of winding them; but, so strong was the compulsion of habit, I do remember thinking bitterly that they ought to be wound and that the register and thermograph sheets ought to be changed. Evidently I performed these tasks; for the instruments were still going next day; and the records, now in the possession of the U.S. Weather Bureau, show that the sheets were shifted at 2 p.m., two hours late. My only distinct memory from that period was arousing and thinking that I was blind. My eyes were open, but I could see nothing. Then I realized that I must be facing the wall. The lantern was out (from lack of fuel, I learned presently), but a dim glow showed in the side of the stove.

There is nothing more panicky than the loss of sight. I shall never forget the agony in Floyd Bennett's voice when we pulled him, terribly smashed up, from the debris of our crash landing. 'I'm done for,' he whispered; 'I can't see anything.' His face was a smear of oil; when I wiped it away and he could see again, the expression that transfigured his face was beautiful.

It is painful for me to dwell on the details of my collapse, particularly as the affairs of Advance Base are now receding into the gentling haze of the past. The subject is one that does not easily bear discussion, if only because a man's hurt, like his love, is most seemly when concealed. From my youth I have believed that sickness was somehow humiliating, something to be kept hidden. But the consequences of this collapse were never to depart during the rest of my stay at Advance Base; and my struggle against the one universal certainty played too large a part in my experience there to be omitted from this account.

I have a pretty clear idea concerning much that happened, almost too clear, in fact. I shall not, however, depend upon memory alone. During the days that followed, I set forth in the diary – as far as I was able – what I knew and remembered. How mutual is the instinct which drives a man alone to pencil and paper, as if his destiny required the right last word and period.

The afternoon ran out its time; though my eyes would not stop aching and the pain would not quit my temples, just lying in the sleeping-bag quieted the hammering of my heart. Gradually my mind cleared, and I tried to reconstruct the events preceding the episode in the tunnel. The exhaust vent over the engine, I decided, must have filled with rime, causing the poisonous gases to back into the tunnel. I was pretty sure that it was carbon monoxide. The instantaneous way I was struck down, the absence of any consciousness of suffocation bespoke these things, plus the symptoms – the splitting headaches, the nausea, the stabbing pains in my body and eyes, the hot and cold rushes of dizziness. What had saved me in the tunnel was the fact of my being dropped as though poleaxed. Since monoxide rises, the air at the bottom of the tunnel must have been all right; and the oxygen entering my blood brought me around.

All this represented a mind groping for bearings. To know I had escaped disaster in one form was only a preliminary step in the process of preparing to avert it in another. The fact was manifest that I was helpless, at least for the time being. I barely had strength to light the candle standing on the tin ledge directly over my head. If so simple a movement could empty me of the little strength that had returned, what chance did I have of bringing in food and fuel from the tunnels, let alone attending to the instruments? I could live many days without food. I could suck snow to quench thirst. But, ill and weak as I was, I could not live long without heat; and the fuel tank had to be filled every three days. Pondering such difficult matters was too much for me; my mind went blank again. When I awakened and looked at my wrist watch, the time was 7 o'clock. I wasn't quite so weak and my body craved water.

So I drew the flashlight from the sleeping-bag and propped it on the edge of the bunk in order to direct the beam towards

the stove. With this to guide me, I slipped from the bunk, clinging to the side for support. Waves of dizziness swept from head
to foot, but after a little while I was able to reach the chair and
push it towards the stove. A little water remained in the bucket
on the stove; I dipped it out with a can. The first swallows my
stomach threw up; nevertheless, I persevered until I had at least
a cupful down. Wondering why my teeth chattered so, I put
my hand against the stove. It was out – no longer than a few
minutes, evidently, else the water would have frozen. *Thursday
... Thursday ... the day to fill the tank.* So the tank was dry,
as was the lantern; and if I wanted to have light and warmth,
both must be filled at once.

The notes which I jotted down a few days afterwards insist
this stranger reeling in the dark acted with the utmost deliber-
ation. Perhaps so. Between the pain and the weakness it was
hard for more than one thought to find a lodgment. I managed to pull on my parka and mittens. Then I lifted the empty
tank from the stand. Holding it by the handle with one hand
and the flashlight with the other, I started into the tunnel. The
nearest fuel drum – by the grace of God equipped with spigot –
was only fourteen feet from the door; but to make the distance
I had to stop and put around my neck the loop attached to the
flashlight so as to free one hand with which to steady myself.
I walked slowly and uncertainly; as, years ago, I had walked
for the first time after being desperately ill of typhoid fever while
on a midshipman cruise to England.

The funnel lay on top of a barrel. I fitted it into the tank;
and, while the tank was filling, I rested on a box. But, though
I had the strength to lift the tank (it weighed about twenty-one
pounds filled to the brim), I could not carry it far. After a few
steps my heart was pounding, and the dizziness returned. I let
go and slumped on the tool box, near the head of the tunnel.
For how long? I really don't know. Long enough, anyhow, to
be shaken by the cold. If I couldn't carry the tank, perhaps I
could pull it, which was what I did – a few feet at a time.
At least, I remember doing that.

Inside the shack, I poured half a gallon or so of the precious
stuff into a pitcher; this would do for the lantern. A lot spilled

on the floor. Presently I succeeded in lifting the tank itself to the stand behind the stove. With that a feeling of relief possessed me for a moment. I could now hold off the cold for at least two days, and maybe three if I economized. Nevertheless, I didn't attempt to light the stove, dreading the effort and knowing that I ought to be in the bunk; but, craving light after the long darkness, I did light the lantern. The light was so cheery that I was encouraged to attempt an observation at 10 p.m. (Actually 8 p.m. my old time; for, a day or two previously, I had advanced my clock two hours, as an experiment in moon-light saving, so to speak.)

That was a mistake. I was able to climb the ladder all right, resting at every rung; I pushed the door back with my head, waited a moment, and then hobbled to the instrument shelter, feeling dizzy and utterly forlorn. I guessed the wind's velocity as being seventeen miles per hour (the register trace shows an actual wind speed of only seven miles), and noted the absence of aurora. But I was unspeakably weak and sick again when I reached the bottom of the ladder. I must sleep, I must sleep, something was saying inside me. In the Escape Tunnel I groped around until I found the box of pheno-barbital pills. With the box in my hand I stumbled to the hut. I got my parka, pants, and shoes off; but the shirt was beyond me. Using the chair as a step, I hung the lantern from its peg above the bunk, then climbed in, weighed down by a sense of complete futility.

The instant the candle died, the darkness dropped like a blow. Sleep was the great hunger; but it would not come, so cruel was the pain in my head and back and legs. As I lay there, the intimation came that I would not recover. Carbon monoxide poisoning is an insidious thing. Once the haemoglobin in the blood stream and the lungs is broken down, it takes the liver and spleen a long time to restore the oxygen-carrying material. Even with the best of hospital care this is a matter of weeks and sometimes months. For me the worst of the cold and the darkest part of the night were yet to come. The sun was nearly three months away. I could not persuade myself that I had the strength to meet it. To some men sickness brings a desire to be left alone; animal-like, their one instinct is to crawl into a hole and lick the hurt. It used to be so with me. But that night, as never before, I discovered how alone I was; and the realization evoked an indescribable desire to have about me those who knew me best. Remembering the meticulous preparations, the safeguards which I had thrown about myself, my soul was bitter with reproaches. My fort had become an ambush. Nothing within the power of the night or cold had made it so. My stupidity was to blame, and this I should have feared before the others.

Even in my stupor I seem to have recognized that the gasolene engine was not solely responsible. The engine dealt the blow which knocked me down, but long before then I had partially perceived a developing weakness. I remembered the notches I had taken up in my belt; the headaches and hurt in my eyes earlier in the month. Maybe the frost in my lungs was a fault. Maybe something was organically wrong with me. But I doubted that these by themselves could have depleted me so much. What reason I could muster indicted the stinking stove as the principal villain. Monoxide poisoning is not necessarily an instantaneous matter. It may be a gradual and cumulative process, brought about by intermittent exposure to the chemistry of the fumes. And the more I thought about the leaky joints in the stove, the more I blamed it.

But all this was shadowy in my mind that last night in May. I wavered between self-recrimination and hopefulness, between pain and an emptiness devoid of feeling. I knew that I was in a frightful mess, one that would involve my family, the expedition, and God only knew whom else. But it was hard to see what could be done about that. I lighted the candle, intending to write certain messages; but no paper was within reach. After a little while I blew out the candle. In my hand was the box of sleeping pills. I was reluctant to take one, not from squeamishness but from the fear that the drug would weaken me further. So, telling myself I would wait until 4 o'clock before resorting to the sedative, I put the box down. Sometime after 3 o'clock I drifted off into a dream of horrors . . .

For two months, Admiral Byrd lived alone on the verge of death from carbon monoxide poisoning. On the radio to his base, he tried to pretend he was all right, because he was afraid his men would risk their own lives in trying to rescue him before the winter was over. But by August they suspected he was seriously ill, and they made an early start to try to reach him. On the first two attempts, they were beaten back by blizzards.

*August 8*
They started again early this morning for the third try – Poulter, Demas, and Waite. The day was clear, the light good, and the cold only so-so. The air was in the minus fifties early this morning, but it warmed up in the minus thirties around midday and is now holding fairly steady just under the minus-forty-degree line.

Charlie was cheerful. 'Keep the lights going, Dick. This time I really think they're going right through,' he said. Well, that remains to be seen. I cannot allow myself to hope again; the drop into failure is too abrupt. The great pity is that I am only half in touch with Little America. I can hear them well enough, but they can't get me. I've already had the transmitter apart once, and I shall have another go at it tonight.

Next day was Thursday. I awakened with the unshakable conviction that this trip, like the others, must inevitably end in failure. Better now than then, I understand why I chose to adopt this attitude; it was a defence mechanism for warding off the terrible wrench of another disappointment. Strangely, I had no true sense of despair; rather, I thought I was being downright realistic. My own personal stake in the outcome of the journey was of dwindling importance. No matter how the trip turned out, whether they reached Advance Base or not, I was convinced that I personally had little to gain; my salvage value was next to zero. Only one thing continued to be important: the expedition's prestige and the safety of the three men between me and Little America.

The weather was not exactly auspicious. Although the barometer was flickering upward, the sky was overcast, and the weather-vane tentatively fingered the east, which is the storm-breeding quarter. The fear grew up in me that either a blizzard

or a fresh onslaught of cold would trap the party midway between Little America and Advance Base. I became like a spectator
at a play. The dangers massing around the principals were
manifest; but, because the resolution lay in the hands of others,
I could not shout a warning.

Evidently the same uncertainty permeated Little America.
When we met on schedule in the early afternoon, John Dyer
sounded hurried and nervous. From what he said, I gathered
that Charlie Murphy was off ski-ing somewhere. Bill Haines
reported in his place. All that I could make out was that Poulter
was getting along quite well. 'How's weather?' I asked. Bill
thought it looked none too good. 'For God's sake, Bill,' I spelled
out, 'tell them to hurry.' If weather were in the making, I
wanted the party off the Barrier.

'I understand,' Bill answered; 'but they'll be all right. They
can take care of themselves.'

Charlie Murphy took over then. Although his voice was
clearer, I lost much of what was said. However, he finally
fixed for my benefit the fact that the stand-by tractor was in
readiness to go to Poulter's assistance, and that in the event
the tractors failed, June and Bowlin could have one of the planes
ready to fly within forty-eight hours. Charlie Murphy and I
had known each other a long time; we had had a close and
deep affection for each other; and, not so much from what he
said, as from what he left unsaid, I sensed the anxiety in him.
'Thanks,' I replied, 'but you must make no mistakes, nor take
chances.'

Afterwards I sat beside the fire, with a blanket wrapped
around my shoulders. I must have dozed, because the next
thing I knew the shack was completely dark. I had neglected
to fill the lantern, which had burned itself out. I groped around
until I found the flashlight. It was time for the 4 o'clock radio
schedule. Sitting in the dark, I heard Charlie telling me that
Poulter was forty-odd miles on his way, and evidently moving
right along. The rest was barely intelligible. I caught a reference
to lights, and then a sentence asking if I needed a doctor. Mani-
festly, Charlie had his own ideas as to the state of affairs at
Advance Base, and no further deception on my part would be

apt to mislead him. Nevertheless, I replied, 'No, no, no.' And on the negative we shut down for the day.

Thereafter the hours fell like chips from a lazy whittler's stick. I paced the shack from the sheer physical necessity of doing something. Once I went topside for a check on the weather. The wind was all but mute in the south, and the sky appeared to be clearing. The cold was coming on again. From a high of 16° below zero around noon, the temperature was again pressing into the minus thirties. I thought: Poulter can put up with that, after what he has been through. Before closing the hatch, I looked north and, I think, said a silent prayer for the three of them.

For supper I had soup, crackers, and potatoes; and, when they were down and promised to stay down, I went to bed. I pondered a long time. The likelihood to which I had blindly closed my mind was virtually a demonstrated fact: namely, Little America had now made up its collective mind that I was in trouble, and Poulter was coming more to help me than to observe meteors. And, if this was truly the case I knew for a certainty that he must be determined to make a run for it, regardless of the condition of the flags beyond the valley of Crevasses. This explained all the talk about lights. Once safely around the crevasses, he was evidently of a mind to steer by compass for Advance Base, trusting to find me by a light which could be seen fifteen or twenty miles away.

I could see the risk in that. Suppose I collapsed entirely. Without a light to fetch him in, Poulter might pass within a hundred yards or so of the Base and never see it. That would be easy to do on a dark night. And if in the hurry they should push too far to the south, then it would indeed go hard with them. True, they knew the position, and Poulter could determine his own location within a mile or two by taking star sights. But taking these in the cold is no simple matter; and, indeed, if the sky was overcast, it would be impossible. In that case, Poulter's only recourse would be to block out an area and criss-cross it until he ran down the base. Meanwhile, more hours would be used up, more gasolene; and the danger from crevasses in an untested area would be multiplied by many times.

Clearly, then, I had a task to do. Instead of being merely a passive objective, I must also be an active collaborator. My job was that of lighthouse keeper on a dangerous coast. I simply had to stay on my feet; and, since my reserve strength was almost exhausted, I must husband the little that remained. There was no sense in frittering it away as I had done in the past, setting off my gasolene pots when Poulter was so far away that he couldn't possibly have seen them. So I drew myself up into the bunk, lighted a candle, and calculated his probable arrival time. At 4 o'clock he was some forty miles and thirty-seven hours out of Little America; his average speed, therefore, was one and a fraction miles per hour. He had eighty miles to go. Even with the best of fortune, he wouldn't be apt to travel faster than five miles per hour. Suppose by the grace of God he was able to make that speed. In that case he would arrive about 8 o'clock in the morning.

This seemed too good to be even possible. But I had to be ready for any eventuality. Therefore, I resolved to have the first kite in the air by 7 o'clock in the morning, and to burn gasolene at two-hour intervals during the day. More than that I could not do; and I was doubtful that perhaps even this was within my scope. Anyhow, I reached out for sleep. It was a long time coming; and, when it came, it was haunted with phantasms of crevasses and floundering men and dancing, far-off lights.

In the morning I awakened with a start. Ordinarily the business of waking up was a long-drawn-out inner struggle between resolution and despair, but this time I was pitched headlong into alertness. I dressed as rapidly as I could, lit the stove, and went slowly up to the surface. It was 7.30 o'clock by the wrist watch. The day was dark. Heavy clouds were heaped up in the eastern sky. From habit I glanced north. And this time I swore I saw a light. To be sure, I shut my eyes. When I looked again, the light was gone. Stars had deceived me on many occasions, and one might have misled me then; I did not think so. The conviction brought an access of strength.

The kite was standing at the foot of the ladder. I hauled it up on a string and soaked the long tail in gasolene, leaving a couple of feet of paper dry at the end. This would be the equivalent of a fuse and give me time to haul the kite into the air before the tail burned up. Then I started down wind with it. There was just a whisper of a breeze out of the southeast. To save strength I crept part of the way. Altogether I went about two hundred feet, the longest distance in many a day. I scooped out a little hole, stood the kite upright in it, and piled snow loosely around the vertical strut to hold it erect. Then, after straightening out the tail, I fired the paper. Although I footed it back as fast as I dared, the gasolene was blazing before I reached the other end of the line.

Not having the strength to run, I had to jerk the thing into the air, pulling in the line hand over hand. The first pull was lucky. A gust of wind caught the kite, lifting it cleanly. I yanked hard, and it skated to a height of a hundred feet. The sight of it swaying against the night, dangling a fiery tail, was very satisfying. It was my first creative act in a long time. The light lasted for perhaps five minutes. Then it shrank to a mere incandescent filament, which finally parted and fell. No answer came from the north. I hauled down the kite and turned to the battery of gasolene signals. I fired two charges in quick succession. Nor did this evoke a response. The frenzy passed, and I stumbled from exhaustion. Too weak to go farther for a moment, I sat down on the snow to think. My lights must have been visible for at least twenty miles. The fact that Poulter hadn't answered meant that he must be still out of sight. Therefore, I could rest from the signalling for at least four hours more.

Back in the shack I paused at the radio and listened for ten minutes or so on the chance that Little America might be on the air. The air was silent. By then the snow had melted in the water bucket. I made a little hot milk, which refreshed me, then climbed into the sleeping-bag, leaving the lantern burning. I dozed intermittently. Several times I thought I heard the scrunch of tractor treads, but it was only creaking noises within the Barrier itself; and several times the singing of the antenna wire in the wind similarly tricked me. At noon I went topside again with my field-glasses. The dawn light was quite strong; I could count at least a dozen flags down the trail, which meant visibility was good for two miles; and a rosy glow suffused the northern quadrant, half-way to the zenith. But nothing moved.

At the regular time I met Little America. Murphy was almost jubilant. Six hours before, Poulter had advised that he was more than half-way around the Valley of Crevasses. Best of all, he had picked up the trail. Indeed, the flags were apparently standing clear. Poulter said that he expected no more trouble; he was over the Hump. 'This is the best news in a long time,' Charlie said. 'We have another schedule with them at 3.45 o'clock. We'll broadcast a report to you then.'

An hour later I pulled myself up the hatch, and fired a can of gasolene. No answer came; but then, I did not expect one so soon. At 4 o'clock Little America was calling in great excitement: Poulter was ninety-three miles south, dead on the trail. 'According to the last report,' Charlie said, 'the generator brushes are giving out, but Poulter is pretty certain that he won't be held up. Good luck to you, Dick. Don't forget to keep the lights burning.' I didn't reply, dreading what would happen if I cranked the generator.

When Dyer signed off, saying he would look for me again in four hours, I tried to collect my thoughts. Charlie guessed that with luck Poulter might be at Advance Base in another eight hours – by early morning at the latest. The prospect was too big to visualize. It was like knowing in advance that you would be reborn again, without the intermediate obliteration of death. Moreover, I thought that Charlie was still overly optimistic. Poulter still had about thirty miles to go. In the 61 hours he had been under way, he had averaged 1¼ miles per hour; and, in the past 24 hours, less than 2 miles per hour. Even at the latter speed, he was still 15 hours distant from Advance Base. So he wasn't apt to arrive much before 7 o'clock in the morning.

Even so, prudence persuaded me to make ready for an earlier arrival. About 5 o'clock I went up the ladder. The sky had cleared considerably, but the grey dawn light had gone, and the Barrier had seldom looked so black and empty. I set off another can of gasolene; as before, no answer came, nor did I expect one. I dropped below and rested an hour. I forced myself to read Hergesheimer's *Java Head*, incidentally; but my mind would not follow the words. At 6 o'clock I was again at the trap-door. And this time really saw something. Dead in the north a beam of light lifted from the Barrier, swept to the vertical, and fell; then it rose again, touched a star, and went out. This was unmistakably Poulter's searchlight, and my first guess was that it wasn't more than ten miles away.

I was inexpressibly happy. With a flare in my hand, I made for the kite, half falling in my eagerness. I made the flare fast to the tail, lit it, and, by repeating what I had done before, I jerked the kite seventy-five feet into the air. The flare burned brilliantly for about five minutes. All the time I watched the north but in vain. The flare died, and I let the kite fall. For half an hour I sat on the snow, just watching. The darkness deepened perceptibly. I knew that I had seen a light, but after all the disappointments I was ready to mistrust anything. What I had to have was a clear-cut decision, one way or the other. This waiting, this coming and going, this uncertainty, were intolerable. This was the seventy-first day since the first collapse. I had endured as much as human frailty could bear.

When I moved to rise my strength was gone. I crawled to the hatch, slipped down the ladder, and made for the bunk. My weariness was infinite. Yet, I could not lie still. Half an hour later I headed topside, halting at every rung of the ladder. You will see their lights close by, I told myself. No lights showed. The Barrier was solid gloom. But they must have seen the kite flare. If they had, then they must have felt no need to make acknowledgement. For I saw nothing, and heard nothing. I fired another can of gasolene; when it burned dry, I ignited another flare, which I planted upright in the snow. Conscious-ness of my own futility added lead to my feet. The minutes went by. At 7.30 o'clock a few stars struggled clear of the cloud rack. Where are they now? Carefully I lighted another can of gasolene, and waited for it to go out. Maybe they have camped for the night. But I knew they wouldn't do that, having come so close. In my pessimism I imagined the worst: a break-down, fire, perhaps they had fallen through a crevasse.

The red trace on the thermograph was working through the minus forties. I was unspeakably disheartened when I picked up the earphones. Charlie Murphy was in the midst of a report. As nearly as I could tell, Poulter hadn't been heard from since 4 o'clock. The earphones fell from my hands. It is a pity that I didn't wait to hear more, for Murphy was trying to tell me that this was in all probability a very good sign; that, having drawn so near Advance Base, Poulter had no doubt decided not to waste time broadcasting, but was pushing on as fast as he could. The fact was that I was at the end of my tether. My mind turned vague; and, when I recovered my faculties, I was sprawled half in and half out of the bunk.

The cold roused me. It was then about 8.30 o'clock. I hitched myself to the top of the bunk, pulled the blankets up, and fell asleep. I slept for about an hour and an half. Then, realizing that I simply must tend to the signals, I drove myself to the ladder. The best I could do was to get half-way up. I lunged back into the shack and tried to think what I could do. Obviously, I needed a stimulant. Remembering what alcohol had done to me the last time I had tried it, I ruled that out. The rest is not wholly clear. In the medical chest was a hypophosphate containing strychnine. Around the bottle was a slip of paper listing the ingredients and the dose – one teaspoonful in a glass of water. The fluid was frozen, but I thawed it in the water bucket. I took three teaspoonfuls in a cup of water, and on top of it three cups of the strongest tea I could brew. I felt lightheaded, but my strength seemed to come up.

Armed with another flare and a length of flexible wire, I pulled myself up the hatch. Temporarily, at least, I had strength to spare. I threw the wire over the radio antenna between two of the poles, made the flare fast to one end, fired the fuse, and then hauled it to the top of the antenna. The light was blinding. When it died out, I blinked my eyes and peered into the north. The fingering beam of a searchlight moved slowly up and down against the dark backdrop of the horizon. It might be another hallucination. I sat down, resolutely facing the opposite horizon. When I stood up and looked again the beam was still fanning up and down. Indeed, I soon made out a second light, fixed and dimmer than the first, evidently a headlight.

This was indeed the world advancing to meet me. In a little while I should see friends and hear voices talking. The escape which for two and a half months had existed only in imagination was now becoming reality. It would be hard to describe exactly what that light did to me. In my whole life I can recall but one comparable experience. That was at the fag end of the transatlantic flight. We had crossed the Atlantic in fog and storm, and on the coast of France ran into a succession of line squalls which gave way to rain and more fog. Although we did reach Paris, we were obliged to turn back to the coast, as that was the only place we could land without killing somebody other than ourselves. Our fuel was nearly gone; the four of us were exhausted; and ahead of us, as certain as death, was a crash landing. And then, in the forty-fourth hour, on the coast of France, we saw a revolving light, which was the beacon of the lighthouse at Ver-Sur-Mer. Well, seeing the tractor's lights was something like that, only this time I had waited longer and suffered more. In that miraculous instant all the despair and suffering of June and July fell away, and I felt as if I had just been born again.

Suddenly the lights disappeared. The car had dipped into one of the shallow valleys with which the Barrier abounds, and the intervening ridge had blotted it out. Therefore the tractor must be some distance off, and I doubted that it would reach me for another two hours. After lighting another can of gasolene – that left only two – and the next to the last flare, I went below, intending to prepare supper for my three guests. I dumped a couple of cans of soup into a pan, and set them on the fire to heat.

When next I peered from the hatch, I saw the searchlight very clearly – so clearly, in fact, that I was able to decide that it was fixed to the side of the cabin. Even then, I decided, they were still five miles off. It would take them another hour to run out the journey. So I sat down in the snow to await the conclusion of this wonderful event. In a little while I could hear on the clear, vibrant air the rumble of the treads, then the *beep-beep-beep* of the horn. But the car was not appreciably nearer. Feeling cold, I went below and huddled beside the fire for a little while. It was hard to sit still when a miracle was being contrived overhead; yet, I compelled myself to do so lest I collapse completely. I looked around the shack and thought how different it would be in a few minutes. It was a filthy mess, and I remember being ashamed that Poulter and the others should find me in such a state; but, while I did make a few feeble passes at the untidy heaps, I was too weak to do much about them.

A few minutes before midnight I went topside again. They had come very close. I could see the bulking shadow of the tractor. As a greeting I set off the last can of gasolene and the last flare. They were just dying when the car stopped about a hundred yards away. Three men jumped out, with Poulter in the centre, looming doubly big in furs. I stood up, but I did not dare to walk forward. I remember shaking hands all around, and Waite insists that I said: 'Hello, fellows. Come on below. I have a bowl of hot soup waiting for you.' If that is really so, then I can only plead that no theatricalism was intended. The truth is that I could find no words to transport outward what was really in my heart. It is also said that I collapsed at the foot of the ladder. I have only a muddled impression of that and a slightly clearer one of trying to hide my weakness. Nevertheless, I do remember sitting on the bunk, watching Poulter and Demas and Waite gulp down the soup and the biscuits; and I do remember what their voices were like, even if I am not sure of what they said. And I do remember thinking that much of what they said was as meaningless as if it were spoken in an unfamiliar tongue; for they had been together a long time, occupied with common experiences, and in their talk they could take a good deal for granted. I was the stranger.

– from *Alone*

LARRY FORRESTER

# Fly for Your Life

Wing Commander Robert Stanford Tuck was one of the most distinguished of fighter pilots in the Battle of Britain. He was credited with shooting down 29 enemy aircraft before at last he was shot down himself over France and imprisoned. By then, he had had so many hair-breadth escapes that his luck, and his skill, had become a legend in Fighter Command of the Royal Air Force. Here is the story of two of those escapes.

As he crossed the coast, far to the north and very high he could see a tremendous tangled mass of vapour trails, and tiny glints of metal ... then the hurtling, weaving fighters, mere dots, flitting in and out of sight, like dust motes in the sun's rays. He advanced his throttle through the gate into 'emergency power' and clambered up frantically to join in the fray. Soon he could distinguish 109s, Hurris, Spits, 110s, a few Ju. 88s ... It was the biggest mix-up he'd seen, an awe-inspiring spectacle that made his throat tighten and produced an odd, damp feeling at the temples and wrists.

Then suddenly, far below him two 88s passed, very close together, striking out for home at sea level. He turned out from the land, away from the main scrap, and with a long, shallow dive got well ahead of them. Then he turned again, due west, dropped low over the water and made a head-on attack.

The port one reared up so violently as the Spitfire's bullets ripped into the cabin that its slender fuselage seemed to bend backwards, like the body of a leaping fish. Then one wing dipped, it cartwheeled and vanished in an explosion of white water. It was exactly as if a depth charge had gone off.

He pulled up sharply into a half-loop, rolled off the top and dived hard after the second bomber. He passed above it, raced ahead, and came round again for another head-on attack.

Tracer came lobbing leisurely at him; from this angle it

wasn't in streaks, but in separate, round blobs, like a long curving chain of electric light bulbs. The stuff was strangely beautiful, the way it glowed even in the broad daylight. At first it was well out of range, but as the two aircraft raced towards each other suddenly he was flying in the broad jet of the Junkers' forward guns, and the tracer seemed to come alive and spurt straight for his face at bewildering speed. He concentrated on his own shooting, and saw his stuff landing on the bomber's nose and canopy.

The enemy's silhouette, lined almost black against the sunlight, remained squarely in his sight, growing with incredible rapidity, and all the time those wicked blue flashes twinkled merrily on it. It came on and on like that, calm and beautiful and stately as a giant albatross, straight and unflinchingly as though it were some purely automatic missile, an unfeeling super-arrow, scientifically, inexorably aimed so as to drive its point between his eyes.

He had the sudden unsettling conviction that this one was different from all the others. This one was more dangerous. It wasn't going to stop firing at him, it wasn't going to break off no matter how much lead he pumped into it.

This one could be death.

All this was happening, all these thoughts and feelings were crowding on him, in the space of a mere two or three seconds. But everything was so clear, so sharply focused. The moment seemed to stand still, in order to impress its every detail on his mind.

The silhouette grew and grew until it seemed to fill the world. He clenched his teeth and kept firing to the last instant – and to the instant beyond the last. To the instant when he knew they were going to crash, that each had called the other's bluff, that they could not avoid the final terrible union.

Then it was a purely animal reflex that took command, yanked the stick over and lashed out at the rudder. Somehow the Spitfire turned away and scraped over the bomber's starboard wing. There could have been only a matter of inches to spare, a particle of time too tiny to measure. Yet in that fleeting trice, as he banked and climbed, showing his belly to his foe, several shells smashed into the throat of the cowling and stopped up the Spitfire's breath. The elaborate systems of pipes and pumps and valves and containers which held the coolant and the oil, and perhaps the oil pump too, were bent and kneaded into a shapeless, clogging mass that sent almost every instrument on the panel spinning and made the Merlin scream in agony.

'With what speed I had left I managed to pull up to around fifteen hundred feet. I was only about sixteen miles out, but I felt sure I'd never get back to the coast.

'I can't understand why that engine didn't pack up completely, there and then. Somehow it kept grinding away. I was very surprised, and deeply grateful for every second it gave me.

'As I coddled her round towards home I glimpsed the 88 skimming the waves away to port, streaming a lot of muck. In fact, he was leaving an oily trail on the water behind him. I had the consolation of thinking the chances were that he wouldn't make it either.'

While Tuck was turning west, the Junkers was staggering uncertainly round to the east. And so they took leave of one another, and went their separate ways, each grievously damaged, neither likely to survive the brief but violent encounter. For a small fraction of a minute they had been face to face, gun to gun, skill to skill. A split-second eternity which, if either pilot were to live a hundred more years, he would be able to recall in greatest detail upon his deathbed. Two men who did not know each other, who almost certainly would never meet again. Yet, if they did survive, though far apart, in their hearts in time they would come to be as brothers, respecting, admiring, cherishing the memory and the mystery of one another as only old enemies can.

At the time, of course, there was no chance or reason to think of such things. At the time, Tuck admits, he was heartily glad to see the Junkers in as poor shape as himself, and he hoped fervently that the German would crash into the sea – which, let's face it, is very probably what happened. It is only now, after the mellowing, decelerating years, as he trudges about his Kent farm that Tuck occasionally finds himself wondering if that bomber reached the coast or 'ditched' successfully, if the pilot is still alive and, if so, what is he like and what is his name and where is his home and does he like his beer and does he remember and does he wonder about me ...?

'I trimmed up and the controls seemed quite all right. The windscreen was black with oil. Temperatures were up round the clocks and pressures had dropped to practically zero. But she kept on flying after a fashion. Every turn of the prop was an unexpected windfall – that engine should have seized up, solid, long before this.

'I knew it couldn't last, of course, and I decided I'd have to bale out into the Channel. It wasn't a very pleasant prospect. Ever since my pre-war air collision I'd had a definite prejudice against parachutes. But the only alternative was to try to 'ditch' her, and a Spit was notoriously allergic to landing on water – the air scoop usually caught a wave and then she would plunge straight to the bottom, or else the tail would smack the water and bounce back up hard and send you over in a somersault. Baling-out seemed the lesser of the two evils, so I opened my hood, undid my straps and disconnected everything except my r/t lead.

'It got pretty hot about now. The cockpit was full of glycol fumes and the stink of burning rubber and white-hot metal, and I vomited a lot. I began to worry about her blowing up. But there were no flames yet, and somehow she kept dragging herself through the sky, so I stayed put and kept blessing the Rolls-Royce engineers who'd produced an engine with stamina like this. And in no time at all I was passing over Beachy Head.

'I began to think after all I might make one of the airfields. The very next moment, a deep, dull roar like a blowlamp started down under my feet and up she went in flame and smoke.

'As I snatched the r/t lead away and heaved myself up to go over the side there was a bang and a hiss and a gout of hot, black oil hit me full in the face. Luckily I had my goggles down, but I got some in my mouth and nose and it knocked me right back into the seat, spluttering and gasping. It took me a little while to spit the stuff out and wipe the worst of it off my goggles, and by that time I was down to well under a thousand. If I didn't get out but quick, my 'chute wouldn't open in time.

'It wasn't the recommended method of abandoning aircraft – I just grabbed one side with both hands, hauled myself up and over, and pitched out, head first. As soon as I knew my feet were clear I pulled the ripcord. It seemed to open almost immediately. The oil had formed a film over my goggles again and I couldn't see a thing. I pushed the goggles up, then it got in my eyes. I was rubbing them when I hit the ground.'

It was an awkward fall and he wrenched a leg and was severely winded. He was in a field just outside the boundaries of Plovers, the lovely, old-world estate of Lord Cornwallis at Horsmonden, Kent, and several people had witnessed his spectacular arrival. The blazing Spitfire crashed a few hundred yards away in open country. An estate wagon took him to the house, where His Lordship had already prepared a bed and called his personal physician. But Tuck, once he'd stopped vomiting, insisted on getting up to telephone base – and once on his feet, wouldn't lie down again. He had a bath, leaving a thick coat of oil on His Lordship's tub, then despite the doctor's protests, borrowed a stick and hobbled downstairs in time to join the family for tea.

But after that, very suddenly, exhaustion took him. They helped him back upstairs and he slept deeply for three hours. When he awoke his leg felt better and his host's son, Fiennes Cornwallis, was waiting to drive him to Biggin Hill, where a spare Spitfire would be available.

'Drop in for a bath any time, m'boy,' said his Lordship.

At Biggin Hill the only accommodation they could offer him for the night was in the station's hospital. The patient in the next bed was the pilot of a Ju. 88 shot down a few miles from the aerodrome that same afternoon. He was very young and very husky, with a shock of wheat-coloured hair, a bright pink complexion and rather dreamy blue eyes. His injuries weren't serious : minor burns on hands and arms, bruised ribs and a cut head. But he'd been badly shaken; all the stiff, Germanic pride had been knocked out of him and he looked rather lost and sorry for himself, like an overgrown schoolboy whose latest prank had misfired and landed him in adult-sized trouble.

Tuck gave him a cigarette. They found they could converse quite well, for the lad had some English, and Tuck's German was passable. After a while Tuck fell silent, thinking how dreadful it must be to be a prisoner of war, cooped up behind barbed wire in an alien land ... Then he noticed that the German, though in hospital-issue nightshirt, was still wearing an Iron Cross, slung on a broad ribbon about his neck.

'I see you've been decorated.'

'Yes, Iron Cross, second class. And that is the ribbon of the Distinguished Flying Cross that I see on your tunic, is it not, Squadron Leader?'

'Right.'

'Why do the British wear only the ribbon? Why not the cross too?'

'I don't know – this is the custom, that's all. Except on very special occasions.'

The German accepted another cigarette. When Tuck had lit it for him he asked: 'How many victories have you?'

Tuck didn't like this at all – it was the one question he'd taken for granted would be left out of this unique discussion. It seemed to him almost indecent. His voice was clipped and cold. 'I'm credited with eleven aircraft destroyed.' He purposely left out the victory he'd added that very day, and several others which hadn't been confirmed and made 'official'. He was wishing to hell he'd never started all this ...

The German pondered Tuck's answer for many minutes in silence, sitting up very straight in the bed, watching him intently, trying to decide if he was telling the truth. Then he began a long series of questions which Tuck answered curtly at first, and then with growing warmth – because they were good questions, from another pilot, about the calling which had taken up both their lives. Soon he forgot his earlier embarrassment and talked as freely and excitedly as he would in his own mess to one of the young replacements.

At the end of it, the German did something quite startling.

Very solemnly, he took the Iron Cross from his neck and handed it to the Englishman.

'Squadron Leader . . . I should like you to have this. For me the war is finished, but somehow I think you have a long way to go yet. It would be very nice for me to know, when I am locked away in the prison camp, that my cross is still flying – still free, as it were. So please take it with you every time you go up. I hope it will bring you luck.'

Tuck didn't want the medal, but the boy was adamant. So, for once at a loss for words, he accepted it, and promised to carry it always.

He left the hospital next morning and never saw the German airman again. Some days later, thinking back on the incident, he realized – with a strange sort of regret that he didn't quite trust, and which he instantly crushed out – that he hadn't even learned the boy's name.

Precisely one week after his parachute escape he was in trouble again. And lucky again.

He had with him Bobbie Holland and Roy Mottram. An un-identified aircraft had been reported off Swansea. A day or two earlier the big oil storage vats at Pembroke Dock had been hit, and they were still burning fiercely. The great pall of smoke reminded him of that first day's fighting over Dun-kerque. Between 3,000 and 4,000 feet there was a solid shelf of white cloud, and running through this was a distinct, oily black ribbon.

Control told them a small coaster coming up the Bristol Channel was being bombed by a Do. 17, and gave them a course to steer. They dived below the cloud and found the ship, but couldn't see the raider. All at once a plume of spray sprouted just off the coaster's port bow. Still they couldn't spot the Dornier, but now at least they knew its approximate position and course. At full throttle they flashed over the ship and climbed through the cloud. The topside was smooth as a billiard table. Still nothing. Tuck called to the others to stay up top, on lookout, then nipped back underneath.

As he broke cloud and circled, he spotted the big, loggerheaded Dornier making another run on the coaster. Another white plume blossomed close by the little vessel. On the deck he could see a group of seamen fighting back gamely with a couple of ancient Lewis guns.

The Dornier saw the Spit curving in at him, and quickly pulled up, into the cloud. Tuck followed him in, overtaking very fast. As the blinding whiteness struck the windscreen he throttled back hard – to stay behind him, with luck to catch the vaguest outline of his tail.

The best part of a minute passed. His straining eyes saw nothing. Then came a series of deafening thuds and the Spitfire kicked and leapt like a startled foal.

Christ, he was being clobbered ... the Hun's rear-gunner must have X-ray eyes! He kicked his rudder savagely, yawing about violently in an effort to get out of the fire, but couldn't. More thuds, more jolts and shuddering. He narrowed his eyes to slits and shoved his face forward, close to the windscreen. If it could see him, then he ought to see it! But – only the whiteness.

Then his port wing lifted joltingly and, glancing out, he noticed a couple of holes in it. He skidded to the right and at once saw, immediately below and very slightly ahead, the shadow outline of the bomber. He'd been sitting almost on top of it! He closed the throttle, dropped down and slid in directly behind it, ignoring the rear-gunner's furious blasts. Then he opened up the engine and edged up on it. From what couldn't have been more than fifty yards he dealt it a long, steady burst. Then he rose a little to one side, and with his guns roaring again gently brought his nose down slant-wise and literally sawed right across it, from starboard engine through the fuselage to port engine and out to the wing-tip. The cloud thinned suddenly, and he could see holes as big as his fist appearing all over it. But at this low speed the recoil of the second burst threw him into a stall, and he went hurtling down into the clear air.

His engine was critically damaged, spluttering and rasping and leaking glycol. But as he regained control and brought the nose up he saw the Dornier plunge vertically into the water, less than half a mile from the little ship it had failed to hit.

He called up Bobbie and Roy and told them the score. Bobbie had gone steaming off somewhere after a shadow, but Roy came swooping down, slid in alongside, and took a good look.

'One helluva mess underneath,' he reported – and he spoke with a chuckle in his voice, as if his leader was a schoolboy who'd just driven a cricket ball through the vicar's greenhouse. 'I say, you're in beastly trouble and no mistake!'

The smashed engine was losing power fast. Tuck decided he was very unlikely to make the shore. It would have to be the 'chute again. Angrily he made ready to depart, sliding back the canopy, undoing harness and oxygen pipe.

'Going somewhere?' Mottram inquired.

Tuck reached out a hand to disconnect the r/t lead, but surprisingly, the engine began to provide spasmodic bursts of power. He hesitated. The shoreline drew closer. Then a last gallant pop or two and the Merlin died. Dead ahead there were sheer cliffs with flat, browned grassland on top – St Gowan's Head. He had about twelve hundred feet. Only seconds to make the decision, and his judgement had better be precise.

He decided he could just make it. He could stretch his glide and set down on the clifftops. The ground looked rough: he'd have to make it a belly-landing.

He held the speed at a hair's breadth above the stall mark and, forcing himself to relax, to be delicate and to 'feel' every inclination of his aircraft, settled down once more to fly for his life.

'Ha! – now you've had it!' cried Mottram after they'd descended another two or three hundred feet. 'Should've gone while you had the chance. You'll never get over these cliffs!'

Tuck shot him a hateful glance. Mottram, no respector of rank, responded with a hoot of laughter and some rapid-fire V-signs. Predicting disaster was his way of giving comfort.

Right up to the last moment the issue was in gravest doubt. Mottram, irrepressibly pessimistic, stayed right on Tuck's wing-tip all the way, until the crippled Spitfire, fluttering in the first tremors of a stall grazed the brink of the cliffs and bounced on its belly on sun-cracked, rutted ground. Then he yelled: 'Jolly good!' and got out of the way.

Only as he wrestled to set her down again did Tuck remember, with sickening apprehension, that he'd undone his safety straps. No time to rectify that now – he could only hope he'd get away with black eyes and a broken nose, not crack his skull ...

Then the tail struck a bump and the Spitfire bounced up again, this time for all of a hundred feet. All hope drained away. Now he would surely stall – a wing would drop, she'd plough in on her back ...

She seemed to stop in mid-air and drop vertically, like a lift, but shaking herself like a dog after a swim. He shoved the stick hard forward and worked the rudder feverishly to try to keep her straight.

Steel bands around his chest, thorax throbbing painfully, damp-faced and dry-mouthed. He was like a man lashed face-upwards on the guillotine – in another instant he would be watching death hurtling at him. But though the needle was for several seconds distinctly below stalling speed, the Spit didn't drop a wing. A creature of true breeding, she kept her poise – and suddenly she was responding, she was flying again, she was gliding down smoothly and steadily!

This time he was able to flatten out with a shade more speed, and consequently more control. Out of the corner of his eye he saw Mottram away to the left, very low, going round in a steep bank, watching him. Then he spotted a hedge across his path just ahead and thought: 'That's handy, that'll break my fall a bit, I'll try to touch down right on it.'

He judged it perfectly. But instead of passing through the leafy barrier, the Spitfire stopped dead, as if she had hit a wall.

She had hit a wall – a dry-stone dyke hidden by the hawthorn. She came from eighty miles an hour to a standstill in about five feet, but Tuck went right on travelling, out of the seat – luckily not upwards, not out of the cockpit, but horizontally, in the general direction of the instrument panel, on and into an ocean of darkness.

When he awoke he could remember nothing at first and couldn't think where he was. No pain, no sound at all. Something was pressing down on his head, though, and there was a strange piece of metal wound around his leg. Odder still, he seemed to be all rolled up in a ball.

He stared at the twisted piece of metal and recognized it as the control column. He looked around some more and found he was sitting on the rudder pedals. Then he knew where he was: he was stuffed into the small space under the instrument panel.

There came to his ears, gradually, a faint hissing and dripping, and he caught a whiff of petrol. That made him wriggle out very quickly. He walked about ten paces and sat down with a thump. It was a great effort to raise an arm and wave to Mottram's low-circling machine, but he managed it. Then he decided to have a nice quiet snooze.

In hospital that night he persuaded a young nursing sister to let him go to the telephone in her office. He was talking to 'Mac', the adjutant at Pembrey, when suddenly he was greatly surprised to find that he couldn't see anything, not even his hand holding the 'phone. He just managed to slur out: 'Well, g'bye, ol' boy, g'bye' and fumbled the receiver back on its hook. Then he did a forward somersault into oblivion.

Post-accident shock, they called it.

— from *Fly for Your Life*

WARD M. MILLAR

# Escape in Korea

Major Ward Millar was an American pilot in the Korean War:
his plane caught fire behind the enemy lines, and when he landed
by parachute he broke both his ankles. In prison camp, a Chinese
doctor put plaster casts on his legs, but they set so that his toes
were pointing downwards. In spite of being so crippled, Ward Millar
was determined to escape.

After the night check that evening, I got out of my pallet,
and, holding on to the wall, pulled myself to a standing position.
Since my feet were tipped down at a sharp angle and the casts
followed the contour of my feet, I found myself standing, in
effect, on my toes, and the edge of the cast dug into the top
of my foot.

The first thing I noticed was that the sharp pains were no
longer present. I stretched one leg out in front of me so that
the foot was flat on the floor and the pressure from the cast
relieved. However, in order to do this, I had to rake my body
back at about a twenty-degree angle. Thus, it was immediately
obvious that to walk in these casts, I would have to lean back
and somehow hold myself up at that angle. I realized this was a
difficult if not impossible proposition. Even with crutches, the
going would be difficult.

Then I had an idea. I gathered up a bunch of rags from my
straw mat and bundled them into a small pad, about the size
of a tennis ball. I took a piece of string and tied the ball to the
underside of my right cast, as a sort of false heel. When I stood
up again, I found, just as I hoped, that the wad of rags actually
served to level my foot. I tied a second bundle under the left
cast, and holding on to the wall for support, slowly moved
around the room. The pressure of the bridge of each cast was
hard against the top of my feet, but I knew that was a minor
difficulty since, after I got away, I could break out a section

of the cast. The important thing was that my ankles did not become unbearably painful or swollen.

I could walk – after a fashion.

The following morning my nurse brought me an unusually fine breakfast, consisting of a Korean dish called *cooksu* – tasty noodles, similar to spaghetti, cooked with vegetables in a half gourd. This was the best meal I had had in my fifty days behind enemy lines, and I managed to talk the nurse out of three helpings. With this meal and the new-found knowledge that I might be able to walk, my spirits soared.

This moment of bliss was rudely interrupted not long afterward when the Chinese officer with the wooden holster came into the room and said, 'Dong-a-li hospital no more. You go Na-han-li.' He explained by signs that because there were fewer patients, our 'hospital' was being closed. Several minutes later some Chinese soldiers came in with a litter, and before I had time to collect any of my escape equipment (the ball of rags, cans, etc.), I was lifted up and carried out of the hut. When I came out of my home of the last six weeks, Ho was standing alongside the road with his uncle. They both smiled and bowed slightly as I went by. I nodded back, and then we rounded a bend in the trail, and Dong-a-li was gone.

I knew from hearing it mentioned before that Na-han-li was not more than three or four miles away, so I was not too disturbed about being moved to other quarters. I worried only that the new 'hospital' might be more heavily guarded. If that were so, I knew I had lost a great opportunity. As we passed across the countryside, I studied it with a new interest, knowing that within a few days, I might actually be back this way, a free man. I made notes of the terrain, particularly the direction in which the ridges ran. Then I noticed something I had not seen before – ripe corn in the fields. Here was a source of food at hand! With a few matches, I could have a roast corn dinner every evening.

Na-han-li turned out to be a small village of about twelve huts, all strung out along a narrow oxcart road. Coming up from the south, we stopped at the first hut, and a man whom I later learned was sort of a civilian head of the hospital came out. He did a double-take when he discovered that a '*Mi-Gwa*' had been delivered to his hospital and he asked me in broken English, 'You American airman?'

'Yes,' I said, 'I fly *pancheesa*.'

He said, 'You speak Chinese?'

'A very little,' I said.

Then the Chinese officer who had escorted me began talking to the hospital superintendent in Chinese. It was impossible for me to catch every word, but I knew enough Chinese now to get the drift of the conversation. The officer explained that I was wounded and that I had to be kept in the hospital at Na-han-li until my legs were healed, after which I should be sent to the P.O.W. camps in Pyongyang . . .

My new 'hospital' turned out to be very much like the one in the other village, that is, a forward staging area, from which, under ordinary circumstances, Chinese soldiers were rotated to the rear every four days. By the time I arrived, however, the monsoon rains had worn the road down to an almost impassable state. The trucks were not able to come in to get the wounded or to bring in food and supplies. Most of the patients had been there for a number of days, and there was a shortage of food.

The hut where I took up quarters was about ten by fifteen feet inside, with two doors and no windows. About eight Chinese slept in the room besides me, two of them atop an old clay stove along one wall. Meals were served twice a day, either by the women nurses or by the male nurse who looked like Robert Montgomery. I soon found we had one luxury here the soldiers in the other villages did not have – a few apples. They were small, hard, and green, but after my limited diet of the last seven weeks, they tasted delicious. I ate as many as I could get.

On the fifth of August, five days after my arrival, the travelling team of 'surgeons', the same I had seen once or twice in the other village, came through. I was quite anxious to get my casts off since I knew I could walk without them, so I grabbed one of the doctors and suggested they had been on long enough.

He was a man with a horse-shaped face. He wore glasses and

carried a U.S. carbine. 'How long have they been on?' he asked in English.

'More than two months,' I said, exaggerating a little, hoping to win my point.

I did. Later that day the horse-faced doctor cut the cast away, little concerned about the fact that all the hairs on my legs were pulled out when he yanked off the pieces of the cast. When at last the painful process was completed, he took my heels and pounded on the bottoms, one at a time.

'Does that hurt?' he asked.

I shook my head, I was relieved, for the test seemed to indicate that at least the bones were no longer broken. But the condition of my legs had not improved; they were still bean-pole size. I pointed to my crazily tipped feet and said to the doctor, '*Bo-how.*' He nodded thoughtfully, then said, 'Try to stand up and walk.'

I swung my legs over the edge of the porch on which I had been laid out, then I inched out until my toes touched the ground. When I put my weight on my feet, my legs trembled, and I heard and felt a weird clicking noise in my left ankle. The situation was bad enough, but I made it look worse, hoping to delay further my transfer to the P.O.W. camp. The doctor said of my feet, 'They will get better in due time. Try to get some exercise.' A husky Chinese soldier carried me piggy-back to my hut.

During the next few days I spent every waking minute trying to improve the condition of my legs and ankles. Most of the day I lay in the hut on my pallet, one leg crossed over the other, propped up in the air, rotating my foot as much as I could, in an effort to work some of the stiffness out of my joint. But progress was not easy to discern.

One day, 'Robert Montgomery' brought me two sticks slightly longer than ski poles and told me to try to stand up and use the sticks as braces. He pretended that he was anxious for me to get well, but I knew his real purpose in making me stand was to get an accurate measure of my height. I am six feet tall and a giant by comparison to most of the small Chinese. He was one of those who was fascinated by my height.

I found I could easily stand up with the support of the sticks, especially since the casts were no longer pressing on the top of my foot. By leaning back at about a twenty-degree angle, I could actually shuffle across the floor with most of my weight carried on the two sticks, like crutches. My feet stuck out in front of me like a cowcatcher, more ornamental than utilitarian.

Later one of the Chinese patients loaned me his pair of canvas tennis shoes. These turned out to be useful in protecting the bottoms of my tender feet, but of little help in supporting my ankles since they had no heels or high tops. Every time I put a little weight on the left foot, I could hear that clicking noise, and my feet seemed to cave in slightly. Even so, I was secretly overjoyed because I now realized that if I could just get my hands on a pair of combat boots, I could – however painfully – *walk* out.

The next time I saw one of the 'nurses', I said, in effect, 'Now that my feet are getting well, you ought to return my boots.' I knew full well that my boots had long since been stolen by one Chinese soldier or another, but since they made such a big to-do about not harming my possessions, I thought I might shame them into finding me another pair. My psychology had some effect; the 'nurse' promised to find me a new pair.

When the doctors got ready to leave, the horse-faced type came to my hut to have a final look at my legs. Several of the Chinese soldiers gathered around, so I took the occasion to express my thanks to the doctor and asked him to tell my 'fellow patients' and the 'nurses' at the hospital how much I appreciated the kindness and helpfulness all of them had shown. I said that I had been deeply impressed, and I hoped that after I got well, I would be able to stay around the hospital for a while, working to repay all these kindnesses. I hoped this might delay my transfer to the P.O.W. camps even longer, but I am not certain that the Chinese were influenced one way or the other.

A week passed, and then another, I ate like a hog, and I could feel my strength returning, bit by bit. This was all to the good, but I still needed the boots, so every time one of the Chinese nurses came into the room, I made a big to-do about them, always bringing up the phony Chinese claims that they did not take P.O.W. possessions. At night I prayed that I would get them.

I guess I literally wore them down, for one day one of the 'nurses' finally said, 'O.K. Have shoes for you. American boots.' When he went away to get them, I thought, Thank God. My prayers have been answered. But when I saw what he referred to as 'boots', was bitterly disappointed. His 'boots' turned out to be an old beat-up pair of four-buckle galoshes – Heaven knows where they came from originally – designed to fit a 10½ shoe. Since I wore an 8½ shoe, and had no shoes, my feet literally swam inside the huge gunboats. I shook my head and frowned, then I tossed the galoshes into the straw alongside my pallet. I made it clear to the nurse that the galoshes were a poor substitute for boots.

It was not until two days later that I realized that the galoshes were exactly what I needed.

The thought occurred to me late one evening while I was lying on my pallet, legs crossed high in the air, griping to myself about the way the Chinese doctors had butchered my feet. If I ever get back to the States, I thought, I will either have to have the ankles rebroken and reset, or get a pair of shoes with some kind of built-in heel. Then suddenly I remembered the galoshes. *There was enough room inside them to build in a false heel! Was it possible?*

I sat bolt upright and rummaged through the straw, searching for the discarded galoshes. When I found them, I looked around to make sure the other soldiers were asleep, and then I slipped the right galosh on my right foot. I wobbled it around to see how much room I would have inside, then I grabbed a bunch of straw, wadded it up, wrapped it in a rag, and placed it inside the galosh over the heel. I put my foot back inside. Now it fitted rather snugly against the top of the galosh. Then I had another idea: if I wrapped my ankle and the lower part of my leg with rags, the upper part of the galosh would also fit snugly and provide some support for my ankle.

Within an hour, I had manufactured a second heel cushion for the left galosh and collected enough rags to serve as ankle supports. Without wasting any further time, I put them all together and snapped the buckles shut. I grabbed my two walking sticks, crawled to the doorway, and then outside for a test run. It was still early, and there was a possibility that some of the Chinese were up, but I knew that if they saw me, I could tell them I had an attack of dysentery and had gone outside because of it.

The trial run was a success. The false heels inside the galoshes allowed me to stand upright. Moreover, the space inside the galoshes permitted a sort of mechanical ankle action by allowing my legs to move with a minimum of ankle bending when I took a step. Using the two sticks as ski poles, I found I could hobble along, at least for short distances. I covered the ten yards to the outhouse in record time, compared to crawling or to my performance in the borrowed tennis shoes. When I got back inside the hut that night, I was trembling with excitement because I knew I now held the secret to escape.

My galoshes had turned out to be a blessing in disguise.

I knew it was important to keep this new discovery absolutely secret because the minute the Chinese found out I could walk, however clumsily, they would either post a guard over me or ship me posthaste to the P.O.W. camps. So, during the daytime, I kept the galoshes hidden under the straw. But at night, after everyone was asleep, I put them on, crawled outside, and hobbled up and down behind the hut, 'getting in shape', so that I would be ready for long-distance travel.

Meanwhile, I began assembling my final 'escape kit', which by then consisted of a handful of rock salt, a few scraps of soap, my piece of towelling, the top of a tin can bent double to form a crude knife, and a small can of tinned meat that one of the soldiers had given me when my stomach trouble had been at its worst. I was saving that until I reached the west coast and open water. In addition, I still had the two hundred *won* stuffed inside the lining of the Mae West, as well as my empty escape vest, G suit, and leather jacket. This was not much equipment, admittedly, but I had one factor that overcame any shortcomings – high morale and confidence inspired by the fact that I was at least able to hobble upright.

This ability was doubly important because the Chinese did not even dream I had it, and therefore I was sure that when I did finally turn up missing, they would be amazed and would perhaps limit their search simply because they thought I couldn't walk. This gave me, in effect, an added advantage.

On the afternoon of 14 August, the rains stopped. Later that evening I heard the lashing of gears and roaring of engines as several Russian trucks skidded through the mud, air brakes hissing, and pulled to a stop outside the huts a little down from my own. Almost immediately there was excitement among the Chinese patients; at long last the trucks had come through to take them to the rear. Soon the word spread down the line: everyone was to be evacuated! The Chinese were jubilant, but my heart sank! Once again, on the verge of escape, I was to be evacuated to the rear.

I knew I had to think fast or I would soon find myself looking at North Korean countryside through the barbed wire of a P.O.W. camp. By the time the nurse came by our hut, I had worked out a stratagem: I told him that I had developed a very bad sore throat. Knowing that they wanted me to be 'all well' when I was sent to the P.O.W. pen, I thought they might delay my departure long enough to give me an opportunity to escape. He seemed very upset about the throat and rushed out to get some kind of white, crystalline powder for me to take. Later he talked to me, felt my forehead to see if I had fever, and agreed that I ought not to be moved while I was sick.

That evening most of the Chinese patients were loaded aboard the trucks. But there was not room enough for all of them, so the decision was made to send one of the trucks back the following evening to pick up the stragglers. The nurse said to me, 'You stay one night. Then go Pyongyang.'

I said, 'O.K.,' but thought to myself: That's what you think. I'm leaving here tonight, and not the way you expect!

The nurse told me to get my possessions together, because he wanted to carry me down to the hut where the straggler patients were billeted. I knew this would make my escape more difficult, but there was nothing I could do about it, so I started picking up my stuff. However, just at that moment, the nurse who looked like Robert Montgomery came in with another white powder, and when he saw me 'packing', he asked where I was going. When I told him, he said 'No, no, you stay.' He did not want me to go out in the damp night air. To obey him was to stay in an empty hut, so I lay back down in the straw, thinking that this was just the kind of confusion I needed.

I suspected that the Chinese nurse who looked like Robert Montgomery would come back about eleven for a final bed check, so I had to delay my escape until after then. While I lay on the straw pallet waiting, I went over my plans one last time.

On the theory that it would be the last direction the Communists would follow in their search for me, I had decided that when I left the village I would travel due north away from U.N. lines. After two days of moving at night and sleeping during the daytime, I would then turn due west, and head directly for the coast, which I figured to reach on the third or fourth night, depending on the speed I could make. If possible, I would steal a boat and sail out to sea; otherwise, I would inflate my Mae West and swim and float with the current until rescued.

I believed the odds for success were in my favour, mainly because I could move far better than the Chinese knew. I figured that on the first night, even though I could not leave before midnight, I would make at the very least, four miles, probably three and a half more than the Chinese would give me credit for. The Chinese, I hoped, would spend the first day searching only in the immediate vicinity of the hospital – looking thoroughly in each hut in the village, the huts in outlying areas, and through the fields and streams. On the second day, they might broaden the search considerably, but by then, I would be at least ten miles from Na-han-li, moving steadily away in a direction they were least likely to search.

At about eleven o'clock, 'Robert Montgomery' came into the hut, filled my water bottle, and gave me another white powder. My throat never felt better, but for effect I grimaced as I swallowed, coughed a couple of times, and groaned, holding my hand to my forehead. The nurse sympathized with me, explaining that the powder would help clear up the infection. He said conditions would be better in the P.O.W. camp in Pyongyang, and that I probably would not get another infection. Then he bade me good night and walked out of the hut. I started getting myself ready immediately.

I dressed hurriedly, putting on my Chinese tan cotton trousers, over which I stretched the half-laced G suit. For a moment I considered removing the suit and throwing it away, but I knew that the rubber bladders inside might be useful as flotation equipment in case I was unable to steal a boat, so I kept the suit on. I zipped up my flying suit, now little more than a jacket, tucked my silk scarf around my neck, and climbed into my deflated Mae West. Then I put on my brown leather jacket, and last, over that, I strapped the many-pocketed escape vest.

I stuffed the pockets of the vest full of various 'escape' items, including the small can of tinned meat, a handful of rock salt, several small green apples, my brass spoon, the chunks of G.I. soap, and the piece of white towelling. Last of all I wrapped rags around the lower part of my ankles, and then buckled on the big, black galoshes, making certain that the straw under each heel was in place and nicely tamped. I felt under my pallet to be sure the two walking sticks were on hand, then I lay back to wait a few more minutes until 'Robert Montgomery' had had time to get to sleep. It was about midnight when I finally got up and hobbled out of the back door of the hut.

In order to have cover as I made my way around the village, I walked straight into a cornfield behind the hut. There was a slight wind rustling through the corn stalks, which served to drown out the scuffing noise I made with the gunboat galoshes and sticks. As I moved along, I looked through the stalks for ripe ears, but there were none. The corn was too young.

I stayed in the cornfield until I had cleared the end of the village, then I cut back and got on a narrow, dirt road that led out to the north. It was my plan to follow roads whenever and wherever possible. The Koreans and Chinese rarely used their roads at night, except the main supply routes near the front, so for my purposes they were comparatively safe. I was afraid that if I tried to move through the hills and fields in the dark, I might fall and seriously twist my ankle. As I walked along, I noticed that my galoshes left enormous tracks, with the 'U.S. Royal' emblem clearly visible.

Though I was now well out of the village, I kept a constant watch for Chinese soldiers, because I was not sure whether or not the hospital was guarded on the perimeter. During my two weeks at Na-han-li, I had seen a great many Chinese soldiers who were not patients. Some of them were attached to a unit that was working on a project in the nearby hills, digging revetments and storage bins. But for all I knew, some of them may have been assigned to the hospital. I hurried on, passing first one and then another hut alongside the road. There were burlap bags stacked on the front porch of the second hut, and for a brief moment I considered foraging in them for food, but I gave the idea up when, thanks to the increasing moonlight, I saw two small, Korean children sleeping on the ground in the yard.

A few minutes later, I spotted what I had hoped I wouldn't – the perimeter guard. There were two soldiers, each with a rifle slung over his back, standing in the middle of the road, smoking. I saw the glow of their cigarettes before they saw me, ducked off the road, and slid down into a drainage ditch. Inching along on my hands and knees, I made my way out to a cornfield that paralleled the road, plunged through the stalks for some distance, then turned and walked north once again, making, in effect, a wide detour of the check point. While in the corn, I searched for some ripe ears, but the field had already been stripped, a fact that caused me some anxiety since I was depending completely on the corn as my food supply. Suppose all the fields were stripped. What could I do about food?

During the second hour of travel, the little strength I had began to leave me. My breath became short, my steps hesitant.

The dull throbbing pain in my ankles, which I had tried to ignore, suddenly became a major problem. I sat down to rest on the shoulder of the road, and took a long swig from the canteen. Then I ate an apple. But when I got ready to get up and go, I realized it had been a mistake to rest. My legs were so stiff that I could hardly get to my feet. An almost overwhelming desire to sleep engulfed my senses, and I thought how foolish it was of me not to have tried to sleep during the previous day.

Somehow, I got upright again and wobbled along, holding on to the two sticks, all the while fighting off a feeling of panic. My God, Millar, I thought, don't give up now. You have gone scarcely a mile. Perhaps not even that. The Chinese will find you if you try to hide here. You must push on. I slogged on, holding an image of Barbara and Adrian before me as incentive. I wanted to take out my cross and pray, but both my hands were riveted to the sticks, so I just prayed to myself, saying the 'Our Father' over and over.

The road, or oxcart trail, dipped down and forded a stream, and having no choice, I waded in. The water pressing against the outside of the galoshes was refreshingly cool and I paused for a moment in midstream to enjoy the sensation. For a moment, I was gripped with a desire to lie down in the water and sleep, somewhat like a man weary in snow, but I fought to stay awake and hurried out of the creek. Time was passing. I still had miles to go before I could feel safe. Moreover, if I did not find corn soon, I would have to go all the following day without food.

After leaving the stream, I struck up a kind of steady pace, albeit a slow one, and moved off down the road. Hardly a minute or two passed before I stopped, my ears fully alert. Was that a voice I had heard? My heart was beating loudly, making a 'cush-cush' noise in my eardrums, but above this I could hear, now definitely, voices, and they were someplace behind me, not too far away. They have discovered my escape already and they are following the galoshes tracks, I thought to myself. What to do?

I plunged down the embankment of the road, flailing my sticks wildly, slipping and sliding, until I came to rest on my hands and knees in soft, damp grass. Then, crawling as fast as I could move, I struck out at a ninety-degree angle to the road. I soon reached a point where I could go no farther, and I collapsed, face down in the wet grass. Absolutely motionless, I waited, listened as the voices came on, and on, and on.

Suddenly out of the oncoming babble, I picked up the unmistakable strains of a woman's voice. What was that? Had the nurses come along with the guards? Logic urged against it. Well then, who? My curiosity was so aroused that I had to take a look, so I very carefully turned my head until I could see the road with one eye. Now the voices were very close, and I saw that they belonged not to Chinese soldiers, but, of all things, to a group of a half-dozen Korean civilians, all dressed in white, each carrying a large straw basket on his head. I watched as the procession went by, wondering who they were and why they were out so late. I could not find an answer to those questions, important as they were to my future plans, but I knew at least one thing: they were not looking for me, and the relief following this realization was enough to make me limp all over.

I waited in the grass at least a half hour to let the Koreans get a head start and to make sure none of their friends were following behind; then I crawled back out on the road and got up rather shakily on my feet. The side excursion had consumed my little remaining strength. I was now so tired I could hardly keep my eyes open or put one foot in front of the other. Sheer fear – or perhaps it was some supernatural force in answer to my prayers – kept me going a few minutes longer, until I reached the edge of another cornfield, which seemed to contain some ripe ears. On the first stalk, I found three, and with much creaking and cracking, I managed to break them off and stuff them in the pockets of my C-3 vest.

Now that I had food, I knew I must find a hiding place because I could go no farther, so I kept in the cornfield, pushing towards a hill that rose out of the opposite end. The two army sergeants, Ward and McPherson, had advised me that the safest place to hide in daytime was on a hill. The Koreans, busy in the fields, or in the villages, came into the hills only

to collect firewood. Somehow – I really am not sure how –
I reached the end of the cornfield and crawled some fifty or
sixty feet up the hill until I came to a group of bushy shrubs
into which I burrowed like a rabbit. I took a long swig on
the canteen and then fell sound asleep.

I woke up a few hours later, at dawn, Thursday, 16 August,
a free man! From my slightly elevated position I could see
some distance through the valley. Breakfast smoke was curling
up from the chimneys of the huts. Several Koreans were already
out in the fields, working between rows of corn and beans.
The road down which I had come was clearly visible, and, so
far, empty. I got out an apple and took a bite, thinking, this is
the crucial day. Within a few hours, or even minutes, the
alarm will be spread and the searching parties will be out,
and the whole countryside will be alerted. I must be very careful.

Not seeing any better hiding place, I went back to sleep,
hoping to build up my strength for the long journey ahead.
When I awoke again, it was late afternoon. I sat up and
peered out. There was no sign of excitement or alarm. The
scene was much the same as before, with Koreans working in
the field, the road empty, and smoke drifting lazily from the
chimneys of the huts. Luck is with me, I thought. The Chinese,
for one reason or another, possibly because they couldn't
believe I had gone far, had not alerted the Koreans. Phase one
of the plan was working. The Chinese would not find me that
day, and therefore I had another night to put distance between
them and myself.

My morale zoomed, and after eating another apple, I began
to feel a little cocky. The thought that I was accomplishing
absolutely nothing by sitting still made me impatient to move
on. Was it safe? I looked out into the valley. There were no
Koreans nearby, certainly none close enough to tell I was an
American. From a distance, I thought, I probably looked like a
Chinese, what with my brown clothes. Would a Korean go
out of his way to approach a man he believed to be a Chinese
soldier? I asked myself. 'No,' I answered out loud. 'Then what's
holding you back?' 'Nothing,' I answered myself again, eyeing the
hill above and mentally laying out a route. Minutes later, I

was on my feet, moving across the partially screened hillside in broad daylight.

The hill was not steep, and I was able to reach the top without crawling, although I found my ankles were more stiff and sore than ever. There were no fields on the other side of the hill, so I dropped down just below the crest and continued walking along the ridge, well out of sight of the farmers. I was quite warm and perspiring heavily, losing valuable salt from my system, so I took off my leather jacket and tied it around my waist the way I used to do in grammar school, unzipped my flying suit at the neck, and put my scarf in one of the pockets. Every two hundred feet or so, I paused and took a swig from the canteen, and every few swigs I took a little salt.

At dusk I stopped again in the cover of the bushes for a good rest. For the first time, I took off the galoshes to inspect my feet and, as expected, found big blisters and raw spots along the top and the heel where they came in contact with the galoshes. I would have given a million dollars for a pair of socks. Lacking them, I laid tassels of corn silk over the raw spots and then packed it throughout the galoshes. Afterwards, I ate my last apple and broke open one of the ears of corn, but it was like unravelling a 'Chinese package', which finally turns out to be nothing. The 'ear of corn' was a tiny thing about five inches long, the kernels not yet clearly formed. Nevertheless, I ate it, soft cob and all. It tasted starchy.

Part of my plan was to get back near the road before it became completely dark, so as soon as all the Koreans left the fields, I got up and pushed on, moving down a hillside into yet another cornfield, where I stopped and ate a half dozen of the miniature ears. Then, thinking the stalks offered as good cover as any, I lay down to sleep until dark. I awoke a few hours later, with raindrops splashing in my face. I got up, picked a dozen more ears of corn, stuffed them inside the C-3 vest, then hobbled out onto the road, and once again headed north.

I walked on in the rain, stopping often to rest or to drink a swig from the canteen. It was a very dark night, and I lost a lot of time hiding from and dodging imagined soldiers.

Later I began to get weak, so I stopped and gobbled a few more ears of corn, since eating seemed to restore my strength, at least temporarily. About midnight it began to rain very heavily, and I thought I had probably gone north far enough to throw off any pursuers who might be foolish enough to be out in this weather, so I cut to the left, following a rough trail, and headed almost directly west. Later, I turned to my left again, and headed southwest or, at least, what I figured was southwest, the direction to the nearest reach of the Yellow Sea. I was very tired, and my speed had dropped off to practically zero miles per hour. In effect, I was pulling myself along by the poles with blistered and aching hands, chanting with each slogging step: 'Slowly, but surely ... slowly, but surely ...'

Somehow, I kept going until dawn Friday. Then I found a group of shrubs shaped like an umbrella, and I crawled under them, prepared to spend the day. I took off my wet galoshes, dumped out the pulverized corn silk, rubbed my feet, and doused them with a little water from the canteen. Then I made a pillow of my Mae West and C-3 vest and lay back comforted by the knowledge that my umbrella-shaped hovel wasn't quite as wet and muddy as outside. Before going to sleep, I took out my wooden cross and thanked God for getting me through one more day and asked His help and guidance through the next. When I awoke at about ten o'clock that morning, the cross was still in my hands, resting between two blisters. I had been too tired to put it away.

I ate a few ears of corn, saving the silk tassel for galosh lining, then peeped out at the country around me to find that I was still more or less up in the hills, surrounded by thick underbrush and rocky ravines. The day was beautiful, bright blue, and the overcast gone. There was no sign of human life – no huts, no fields, no people, no noise, save the chirping of birds. Where was I? Which way was the Yellow Sea? Navigation in the air, with charts, computers, and radio aids, was reasonably easy. But now, down on the ground moving across hills at a snail's pace, my visibility reduced to a few feet, I was uncertain, not to say lost, and haunted by the thought that perhaps an inlet or bay of the Yellow Sea lay only a few miles away, hidden from my view by the hills.

There was only one answer to this; in spite of my limited ability to move, especially up, I simply had to climb a high hill and take my bearings, I looked around me. About half a mile away in the north, I saw a cone-shaped, tree-covered knob jutting up into the sky. I judged the hill to be about eleven or twelve hundred feet, not much, but perhaps enough to provide the information and intelligence I needed. There seemed to be little danger of being seen in these hills, so feeling I could not afford to lose a minute of time, I made the decision to move out and climb the hill that very day. I ate a few more ears of corn to give me added strength, put on my galoshes and vests, and then I was on my way.

The hill turned out to be much steeper than it looked from a distance, and I had a very difficult time climbing it. This is the procedure I used: First, I dug both sticks into the hard ground, using them like alpenstocks, after which I put my right foot forward, about one good step. Then, leaning back on the sticks, I brought my left foot alongside my right foot, and gave a big push, enough to swing myself over the balance point. As I swung forward, I pulled the sticks out of the ground, and jabbed them in front of me so that I would not fall forward on my face. Then I resumed the starting position again.

About midday, when I was half-way up the hill, I stopped on a grassy plateau and stretched out to rest, falling asleep as usual. I was not worried about cover or concealment, because I knew no Korean in his right mind would climb the hill on such a hot day. It was late in the afternoon when I awoke. I picked up my sticks and pushed on, crawling the steep rise of the last hundred feet on my hands and knees. I finally reached the summit about five o'clock in the afternoon. I sat down on a rocky ledge and dangled my feet over the side, observing the broad expanse of countryside with more than the casual tourist's interest.

I realized immediately that there was something drastically wrong with my dead-reckoning navigation. There was no water to the west or southwest – only rolling hills as far as the eye could see! Where was I? Was I really in the middle of Korea, some seventy miles from the coast? Was it possible?

Just at that moment, a flight of four United States Air Force F-84 jets whistled overhead, heading north. I watched them as they flew on a few miles, then turned abruptly and began circling. Suddenly the sky around them was dotted with black puffs of smoke – flak. The planes dove down one at a time on some target hidden from my view by a hill, and I heard the bombs as they went off – B O O M – B O O M – B O O M ! Several minutes later after further attacks the planes, pursued by the puffs of black, climbed out, formed up, and then flew south, passing directly over me. I waved, knowing full well it was futile and they would never see me. In less than twenty minutes they would be landing at Taegu. How long would it take me?

It took him a month. He never found the sea, but a Christian North Korean helped him to signal to an American plane, and a helicopter came in and picked him up under fire.

– from *Valley of the Shadow*

# FRIDTJOF NANSEN

# Escape from the Arctic

In 1893, the Norwegian explorer Fridtjof Nansen, with a crew of twelve men, sailed to the Arctic in the ship *Fram*. He had designed the *Fram* to resist the pressure of pack ice, and his place was to let the ship be iced in, and then drift with the ice across the Arctic Ocean.

They drifted for two years. In the spring of 1895, Nansen left the ship, with one companion called Johansen, to travel by dog-sledge towards the North Pole and then back to the island of Spitzbergen. He reached a point nearer the Pole than anyone had been before, but he failed to reach Spitzbergen, and he and Johansen had to spend another winter in a hut which they built of rocks and walrus hides on an unknown island.

It is quite hard to realize nowadays how isolated explorers could be before the days of radio or aircraft. By the following spring, Nansen and Johansen had heard nothing of the world for three whole years, and had not seen another human being since they left the *Fram* a year before. When the ice broke up, they left their hut and began to try to sail towards the south, in two kayaks lashed together, hoping to find a land they would recognize.

In the evening we put in to the edge of the ice, so as to stretch our legs a little; they were stiff with sitting in the kayaks all day, and we wanted to get a little view over the water to the west, by ascending a hummock. As we went ashore the question arose as to how we should moor our precious vessels.

'Take one of the braces,' said Johansen; he was standing on the ice.

'But is it strong enough?'

'Yes,' he answered; 'I have used it as a halyard on my sledge-sail all the time.'

'Oh, well, it doesn't require much to hold these light kayaks,' said I, a little ashamed of having been so timid, and I moored them with the halyard, which was a strap cut from a raw walrus-hide. We had been on the ice a little while, moving up and down close to the kayaks. The wind had dropped considerably, and seemed to be more westerly, making it doubtful whether we could make use of it any longer, and we went up on to a hummock close by to ascertain this better. As we stood there, Johansen suddenly cried:

'I say! The kayaks are adrift!'

We ran down as hard as we could. They were already a little way out, and were drifting quickly off; the painter had given way.

'Here, take my watch!' I said to Johansen, giving it to him; and as quickly as possible I threw off some clothing, so as to be able to swim more easily. I did not dare to take everything off, as I might so easily get cramp. I sprang into the water, but the wind was off the ice, and the light kayaks, with their high rigging, gave it a good hold. They were already well out, and were drifting rapidly. The water was icy cold, it was hard work swimming with clothes on, and the kayaks drifted farther and farther, often quicker than I could swim. It seemed more than doubtful whether I could manage it. But all our hope was drifting there; all we possessed was on board; we had not even a knife with us; and whether I got cramp and sank here, or turned back without the kayaks, it would come to pretty much the same thing; so I exerted myself to the utmost. When I got tired I turned over, and swam on my back, and then I could see Johansen walking restlessly up and down on the ice. Poor lad! He could not stand still, and thought it dreadful not to be able to do anything. He had not much hope that I could do it, but it would not improve matters in the least if he threw himself into the water too. He said afterwards that these were the worst moments he had ever lived through. But when I turned over again, and saw that I was nearer the kayaks, my courage rose, and I redoubled my exertions. I felt, however, that my limbs were gradually stiffening and losing all feeling, and I knew that in a short time I should not be able to move them. But there was not far to go now; if I could only hold out a little longer, we should be saved – and I went on. The strokes became more and more feeble, but the distance became shorter and shorter, and I began to think I should reach the kayaks. At last I was able to stretch out my hand to the snowshoe, which lay across the sterns; I grasped it, pulled myself in to the edge of the kayak – and we were saved. I tried to pull myself up, but the whole of my body was so stiff with cold, that this was an impossibility. For a moment I thought that after all it was too late; I was to get so far, but not be able to get in. After a little, however, I managed to swing one leg on to the edge of the sledge which lay on the deck and in this way managed to tumble up. There I sat, but so stiff with cold, that I had difficulty in paddling. Nor was it easy to paddle in the double vessel, where I first had to take one or two strokes on one side, and then step into the other kayak to take a few strokes on the other side. If I had been able to separate them, and row in one while I towed the other, it would have been easy enough; but I could not undertake that piece of work, for I should have been stiff before it was done; the thing to be done was to keep warm by rowing as hard as I could. The cold had robbed my whole body of feeling, but when the gusts of wind came they seemed to go right through me as I stood there in my thin, wet woollen shirt. I shivered, my teeth chattered, and I was numb almost all over; but I could still use the paddle, and I should get warm when I got back on to the ice again. Two auks were lying close to the bow, and the thought of having auk for supper was too tempting; we were in want of food now. I got hold of my gun, and shot them with one discharge. Johansen said afterwards that he started at the report thinking some accident had happened, and could not understand what I was about out there but when he saw me paddle and pick up two birds he thought I had gone out of my mind. At last I managed to reach the edge of the ice, but the current had driven me a long way from our landing-place. Johansen came along the edge of the ice, jumped into the kayak beside me, and we soon got back to our place. I was undeniably a good deal exhausted, and could barely manage to crawl on land. I could scarcely stand, and while I shook and trembled all over Johansen had to pull off the wet things I had on, put on the few dry ones I still had in reserve, and spread the sleeping bag out upon the ice. I packed myself well into it, and he covered me with the sail and everything he could find to keep out the cold air. There I lay shivering for a long time, but gradually the warmth began to return to my body. For some time longer, however, my feet had no more feeling in them than icicles, for they had been partly naked in the water. While Johansen put up the tent and prepared supper, consisting of my two auks, I fell asleep. He let me sleep quietly, and when I awoke, supper had been ready for some time, and stood simmering over the fire. Auk and hot soup soon effaced the last traces of my swim. During the night my clothes were hung out to dry, and the next day were all nearly dry again.

As the tidal current was strong here, and there was no wind for sailing, we had to wait for the turn of the tide, so as not to have the current against us; and it was not until late the following evening that we went on again. We paddled and got on well until towards morning (June 14th), when we came to some great herds of walrus on the ice. Our supply of meat was exhausted but for some auks we had shot, and we had not many pieces of blubber left. We would rather have had a bear, but as we had seen none lately, it was perhaps best to supply ourselves here. We put in, and went up to one herd behind a hummock. We preferred young ones, as they were much easier to manipulate; and there were several here. I first shot one quite small, and then another. The full-grown animals started up at the first report, and looked round; and at the second shot the whole herd began to go into the water. The mothers, however, would not leave their dead young ones. One sniffed at its young one, and pushed it, evidently unable to make out what was the matter; it only saw the blood spurting from its head. It cried and wailed like a human being. At last, when the herd began to plunge in, the mother pushed her young one before her towards the water. I now feared that I should lose my booty, and ran forward to save it; but she was too quick for me. She took the young one by one fore-leg, and disappeared with it like lightning into the depths. The other mother did the same. I hardly knew how it had all happened, and remained standing at the edge looking down after them. I thought the young ones must rise to the surface again, but there was nothing to be seen. They had disappeared for good; the mothers must have taken them a long way. I then went towards another herd, where there were also young ones, and shot one of them; but, made wiser by experience, I shot the mother too. It was a touching sight to see her bend over her dead young one before she was shot, and even in death she lay holding it with one fore-leg. So now we had meat and blubber enough to last a long time, and meat, too, that was delicious, for the side of young walrus tastes like loin of mutton. To this we added a dozen auks, so our larder was now well furnished with good food; and if we needed more, the water was full of auks and other food, so there was no dearth.

The walruses here were innumerable. The herds that had been lying on the ice, and had now disappeared, were large; but there had been many more in the water outside. It seemed to seethe with them on every side, great and small; and when I estimate their number to have been at least 300, it is certainly not over the mark.

At 1.30 the next morning (Monday, June 15th) we proceeded on our way in beautifully calm weather. As walruses swarmed on all sides, we did not much like paddling singly, and for some distance lashed the kayaks together; for we knew how obtrusive these gentlemen could be. The day before they had come pretty near, popped up close beside my kayak, and several times followed us closely a long distance, but without doing us any harm. I was inclined to think it was curiosity, and that they were not really dangerous; but Johansen was not so sure of this. He thought we had had experience to the contrary, and urged that at any rate caution could do no harm. All day long we saw herds, that often followed us a long way, pressing in round the kayaks. We kept close to the edge of the ice; and if any came too near, we put in, if possible, on an ice-foot. (The ice-foot is the part of a floe which often projects into the water under the surface. It is formed through the thawing of the upper part of the ice in the summer-time by the warmer surface layer of the sea.)

I wrote in my diary: 'Towards morning we rowed for some time without seeing any walrus, and now felt more secure. Just then we saw a solitary rover pop up a little in front of us.

Johansen, who was in front at the time, put in to a sunken ledge of ice; and although I really thought that this was caution carried to excess, I was on the point of following his example. I had not got so far, however, when suddenly the walrus shot up beside me, threw itself on to the edge of the kayak, took hold farther over the deck with one fore-flipper, and as it tried to upset me aimed a blow at the kayak with its tusks. I held on as tightly as possible, so as not to be upset into the water, and struck at the animal's head with the paddle as hard as I could. It took hold of the kayak once more, and tilted me up, so that the deck was almost under water, then let go, and raised itself right up. I seized my gun, but at the same moment it turned round and disappeared as quickly as it had come. The whole thing had happened in a moment, and I was just going to remark to Johansen that we were fortunate in escaping so easily from that adventure, when I noticed that my legs were wet. I listened, and now heard the water trickling into the kayak under me. To turn and run her on to the sunken ledge of ice was the work of a moment, but I sank there. The thing was to get out and on to the ice, the kayak all the time getting fuller. The edge of the ice was high and loose, but I managed to get up, and Johansen, by tilting the sinking kayak over to starboard, so that the leak came above the water, managed to bring her to a place where the ice was low enough to admit of our drawing her up. All I possessed was floating about inside, soaked through. What I most regret is that the water has got into the photographic apparatus, and perhaps my precious photographs are ruined.

'So here we lie, with all our worldly goods spread out to dry and a kayak that must be mended before we can face the walrus again. It is a good big rent that he has made, at least six inches long; but it is fortunate that it was no worse. How easily he might have wounded me in the thigh with that tusk of his! And it would have fared ill with me if we had been farther out, and not just at such a convenient place by the edge of the ice, where there was a sunken ledge. The sleeping-bag was soaking wet; we wrung it out as well as we could, turned the hair outside, and have spent a capital night in it.'

On the evening of the same day, I wrote: 'Today I have

patched my kayak, and we have gone over all the seams in both kayaks with stearine; so now we hope we shall be able to go on in quite sound boats. In the meantime the walruses are lying outside, staring at us with their great, round eyes, grunting and blowing, and now and then clambering up on the edge of the ice, as though they wanted to drive us away.'

'Tuesday, June 23rd.

> "Do I sleep? do I dream?
> Do I wonder and doubt?
> Are things what they seem?
> Or is visions about?"

'What has happened? I can still scarcely grasp it. How incessant are the vicissitudes in this wandering life! A few days ago swimming in the water for dear life, attacked by walrus, living the savage life which I have lived for more than a year now, and sure of a long journey before us, over ice and sea, through unknown regions, before we should meet with other human beings – a journey full of the same ups and downs, the same disappointments, that we have become so accustomed to – and now living the life of a civilized European, surrounded by everything that civilization can afford of luxury and good living, with abundance of water, soap, towels, clean, soft woollen clothes, books, and everything that we have been sighing for all these weary months.

'It was past midday on June 17th when I turned out to prepare breakfast. I had been down to the edge of the ice to fetch salt water, had made up the fire, cut up the meat, and put it in the pot, and had already taken off one boot preparatory to creeping into the bag again, when I saw that the mist over the land had risen a little since the preceding day. I thought it would be as well to take the opportunity of having a look round, so I put on my boot again, and went up on to a hummock near to look at the land beyond. A gentle breeze came from the land, bearing with it a confused noise of thousands of bird-voices from the mountain there. As I listened to these sounds of life and movement, watched flocks of auks flying to and fro above my head, and as my eye followed the line of coast, stopping at

the dark, naked cliffs, glancing at the cold, icy plains and gla-
ciers in a land which I believed to be unseen by any human
eye and untrodden by any human foot, reposing in arctic maj-
esty behind its mantle of mist – a sound suddenly reached my
ear, so like the barking of a dog, that I started. It was only a
couple of barks, but it could not be anything else. I strained my
ears, but heard no more, only the same bubbling noise of thousands of birds. I must have been mistaken, after all; it was only
birds I had heard; and again my eye passed from sound to island
in the west. Then the barking came again, first single barks,
then full cry; there was one deep bark, and one sharper; there
was no longer any room for doubt. At that moment, I remembered having heard two reports the day before, which I thought
sounded like shots, but I had explained them away as noises in
the ice. I now shouted to Johansen that I heard dogs farther in-
land. Johansen started up from the bag where he lay sleeping,
and tumbled out of the tent. "Dogs?" He could not quite take
it in, but had to get up and listen with his own ears, while I got
breakfast ready. He very much doubted the possibility of such
a thing, yet he fancied once or twice that he heard something
which might be taken for the barking of dogs; but then it was
drowned again in the bird-noises, and, everything considered,
he thought that what I had heard was nothing more than that.
I said he might believe what he liked, but I meant to set off as
quickly as possible, and was impatient to get breakfast swallowed. I had emptied the last of the Indian meal into the soup,
feeling sure that we should have farinaceous food enough by the
evening. As we were eating we discussed who it could be,
whether our countrymen or Englishmen. If it was the English
expedition to Franz Josef Land which had been in contempla-
tion when we started, what should we do?

' "Oh, we'll just have to remain with them a day or two," said
Johansen, "and then we'll have to go on to Spitzbergen, else it
will be too long before we get home."

'We were quite agreed on this point; but we would take care
to get some good provisions for the voyage out of them. While
I went on, Johansen was to stay behind and mind the kayaks,
so that we should run no risk of their drifting away with the

ice. I got out my snowshoes, glass, and gun, and was ready. Before starting, I went up once more to listen, and look out a road across the uneven ice to the land. But there was not a sound like the barking of dogs, only noisy auks, harsh-toned little auks, and screaming kittiwakes. Was it these, after all, that I had heard? I set off in doubt. Then in front of me I saw the fresh track of an animal. They could hardly have been made by a fox, for if they were, the foxes here must be bigger than any I had ever seen. But dogs? Could a dog have been no more than a few hundred paces from us in the night without barking, or without our having heard it? It seemed scarcely probable; but whatever it was, it could never have been a fox. A wolf, then? I went on, my mind full of strange thoughts, hovering between certainty and doubt. Was all our toil, were all our troubles, privations, and sufferings, to end here? It seemed incredible, and yet – Out of the shadowland of doubt, certainty was at last beginning to dawn. Again the sound of a dog yelping reached my ear, more distinctly than ever; I saw more and more tracks which could be nothing but those of a dog. Among them were foxes' tracks and how small they looked! A long time passed, and nothing was to be heard but the noise of the birds. Again arose doubt as to whether it was all an illusion. Perhaps it was only a dream. But then I remembered the dogs' tracks; they, at any rate, were no delusion. But if there were people here, we could scarcely be on Gillies Land or a new land, as we had believed all the winter. We must after all be upon the south side of Franz Josef Land, and the suspicion I had had a few days ago was correct, namely, that we had come south through an unknown sound and out between Hooker Island and Northbrook Island, and were now off the latter, in spite of the impossibility of reconciling our position with Payer's map.

'It was with a strange mixture of feelings that I made my way in towards land among the numerous hummocks and inequalities. Suddenly I thought I heard a shout from a human voice, a strange voice, the first for three years. How my heart beat, and the blood rushed to my brain, as I ran up on to a hummock, and hallooed with all the strength of my lungs. Behind that one human voice in the midst of the icy desert, this one message from life, stood home and she who was waiting there; and I saw nothing else as I made my way between bergs and ice-ridges. Soon I heard another shout, and saw, too, from an ice-ridge, a dark form moving among the hummocks farther in. It was a dog; but farther off came another figure, and that was a man. Who was it? Was it Jackson or one of his companions, or was it perhaps a fellow countryman? We approached one another quickly; I waved my hat: he did the same. I heard him speak to the dog, and I listened. It was English, and as I drew nearer I thought I recognized Mr Jackson, whom I remembered once to have seen.

'I raised my hat; we extended a hand to one another, with a hearty "How do you do?" Above us a roof of mist, shutting out the world around, beneath our feet the rugged, packed drift-ice, and in the background a glimpse of the land, all ice, glacier, and mist. On one side the civilized European in an English check suit and high rubber water-boots, well shaved, well groomed, bringing with him a perfume of scented soap, perceptible to the wild man's sharpened senses; on the other side the wild man, clad in dirty rags, black with oil and soot, with long, uncombed hair and shaggy beard, black with smoke, with a face in which the natural fair complexion could not possibly be discerned through the thick layer of fat and soot which a winter's endeavours with warm water, moss, rags, and at last a knife had sought in vain to remove. No one suspected who he was or whence he came.

'Jackson : "I'm immensely glad to see you."
'"Thank you, I also."
'"Have you a ship here?"
'"No; my ship is not here."
'"How many are there of you?"
'"I have one companion at the ice-edge."
'As we talked, we had begun to walk in towards land. I took it for granted that he had recognized me, or at any rate understood who it was that was hidden behind this savage exterior, not thinking that a total stranger would be received so heartily. Suddenly, he stopped, looked me full in the face, and said quickly : –

'"Aren't you Nansen?"

'"Yes, I am."

'"By Jove! I am glad to see you!"

'And he seized my hand and shook it again, while his whole face became one smile of welcome, and delight at the unexpected meeting beamed from his dark eyes.

'"Where have you come from now?" he asked.

'"I left the *Fram* in 84° N. lat., having drifted for two years, and I reached the 86° 15′ parallel, where we had to turn and make for Franz Josef Land. We were, however, obliged to stop for the winter somewhere north here, and are now on our route to Spitzbergen."

'"I congratulate you most heartily. You have made a good trip of it, and I am awfully glad to be the first person to congratulate you on your return."

'Once more he seized my hand, and shook it heartily. I could not have been welcomed more warmly; that handshake was more than a mere form. In his hospitable English manner, he said at once that he had "plenty of room" for us, and that he was expecting his ship every day. By "plenty of room" I discovered afterwards that he meant that there were still a few square feet on the floor of their hut that were not occupied at night by himself and his sleeping companions. But "heart-room makes house-room", and of the former there was no lack. As soon as I could get a word in, I asked how things were getting on at home, and he was able to give me the welcome intelligence that my wife and child had both been in the best of health when he left two years ago . . .

'Then we arrived at the house, a low Russian timber hut, lying on a flat terrace, an old shore-line, beneath the mountain, and 50 feet above the sea. It was surrounded by a stable and four circular tent-houses, in which stores were kept. We entered a comfortable, warm nest in the midst of these desolate, wintry surroundings, the roof and walls covered with green cloth. On the walls hung photographs, etchings, photolithographs, and shelves everywhere, containing books and instruments; under the roof clothes and shoes hung drying, and from the little stove in the middle of the floor of this cosy room the warm coal fire shone out a hospitable welcome. A strange feeling came over me as I seated myself in a comfortable chair in these unwonted surroundings. At one stroke of changing fate, all responsibility, all troubles, were swept away from a mind that had been oppressed by them during three long years; I was in a safe haven, in the midst of the ice, and the longings of three years were lulled in the golden sunshine of the dawning day. My duty was done: my task was ended; now I could rest, only rest and wait.'

– from *Farthest North*

# ACKNOWLEDGEMENTS

Acknowledgements and thanks are due to the following authors and publishers for the use of copyright material:

Messrs. Gerald Duckworth & Co. Ltd for the extract from SALT WATER THIEF by E. O. Hauge, translated by Malcolm Munthe; Hodder & Stoughton Ltd, and the Executors of the late Captain C. O. Jennings for AN OCEAN WITHOUT SHORES by C. O. Jennings; The Hamlyn Publishing Group Ltd, for *I Escape from the Boers* from MY EARLY LIFE by Winston S. Churchill; Evans Brothers Ltd and E. P. Dutton & Co. Inc., New York, for an extract from THE SMALL WOMAN by Alan Burgess. Copyright © 1957 by E. P. Dutton & Co. Inc. Reprinted by permission of the publishers; G. P. Putnam's Sons, New York, for the extract from ALONE by Richard E. Byrd. Copyright © 1938 by Richard E. Byrd, renewed 1966 by Marie A. Byrd; Frederick Muller Ltd, and David Higham Associates Ltd, for the extract from FLY FOR YOUR LIFE by Larry Forrester; David McKay Company Inc., New York, for the extract from VALLEY OF THE SHADOW by Ward M. Millar.